Teaching Out of the Box

I thoroughly enjoyed Teaching Out of the Box. Lots of good ideas. I think it will be a winner for teachers looking for creative ideas. — Jerry Ray, Ed.D., Principal, Los Alisos Intermediate School, Mission Viejo, CA   .

A clever, witty and intelligent piece of work. Amusing and passionate and a MUST for educators. — Joseph Kawaja, MS, Marriage and Family Therapist/#MFC 9335, Specializing in the Treatment of Individuals and Adolescents

The reader will both enjoy and benefit from this book. Author Stan Cody, a veteran teacher, reveals his formula for success – how to make teaching and learning fun while achieving lasting results. Stan brings life to lessons as he connects students with history. Through divergent approaches he motivates students to learn through demonstration and then by doing. Teaching Out of the Box is a worthwhile read for the insight and ideas it provides into teaching American history. Thanks to Stan Cody for sharing his exciting methods. — Don Brann, Ed.D., Superintendent, Wiseburn School District, Hawthorne, CA

Teaching Out of the Box

A Teacher's Guide to Making History Fun...and More

Stan Cody

Stan Cody Publishing
Laguna Hills, California

Publisher's Note: As we constructed the contents of *Teaching Outside the Box,* we made every attempt to include only
original material or to publish the sources of material that was
not original. If we have inadvertently published information
without proper attribution, we invite you to contact us so we
can set the record straight in future editions.

ISBN 0-9778222-0-6
ISBN 978-0-9778222-0-1

Library of Congress Control Number: 2006901567

Published by:
Stan Cody Publishing
25851 Treetop Road
Laguna Hills, CA 92653
www.StanCody.com

Printed in the United States of America

Cover design by Michael D. Wheary, Foresight Design

Interior illustrations by James McLean

Typesetting and production by Wordpix Solutions, Buena
Park, California, Wordpix.com

Note: Quantity discounts on 20 or more books are available
to schools, organizations and the retail trade. The publisher

Table of Contents

Forward

Creative innovation is the gospel of Stan Cody, one of the most dynamic teachers I ever had the pleasure of working with. He truly embodied the concept of "teaching out of the box".

For ten years, Stan taught under my supervision at two schools in the El Segundo Unified School District in Southern California. During that time I personally observed Stan as he implemented the dynamic techniques and practices he describes in this book.

Stan did not fit the typical mold of a classroom teacher. While at times he did practice some of the so-called "techniques and standards of teaching," he more often embarked on his own ideas of what classroom learning is all about. As you read through *Teaching Out of the Box*, you will vividly understand the techniques that made him such an excellent educator.

Stan's methods center around creating an environment that keeps students interested and excited about learning. There was rarely a dull moment in his classroom, and if there was one, he would quickly shift gears and embark on a new strategy. He was always developing ideas to liven up the classroom. I remember a time when Stan came into my office to ask permission to take some of his students fishing as part of a science project, the objective of which was to bring their catch back to the classroom for dissection. While it was an unusual request, I had no doubt that it would allow Stan's students to learn more about fish anatomy than they ever would out of a book, and I granted him permission for the project.

To many of Stan's colleagues, he was a maverick teacher. Schedules rarely fit the learning process, so he rarely followed them. In fact, when things got dull, it was not uncommon for him to take his students outside, perhaps for a wake-up volleyball game or similar activity. During recess and lunch breaks, you could always find him on the playground working with the students – not just his students, but students from other classes too. You would observe him teaching them volleyball, basketball and softball. I sometimes had to deal with other teachers' complaints about Stan's irregular scheduling and working with the students during teacher break time. I should state that his scheduling never interfered with other teachers' use of equipment. When I got complaints, I would just say, "Leave him alone." When testing time came around, Stan's students shone far and above the students of other classes. Many times, members of his class received higher scores than the accelerated students in other classes.

Students in Stan's classes responded very well to his teaching, and the parents of his students were very positive about his practices. To this day, many years later, I still get feedback from parents and students whose lives were changed by the wonderfully creative teaching of Stan Cody.

Stan made learning fun for his students. As you read *Teaching Out of the Box*, you will be inspired by his ideas and practices!

March 1, 2006

Santo J. Prete
Principal, Imperial Street Elementary School,
Richmond Street Elementary School, El Segundo
Unified School District, El Segundo, California

Acknowledgments

I'd like to thank my family for their wonderful listening skills. I bent their ears many times through the years with my mnemonics, timelines and character costumes, all in good fun and practicing for my students.

Deepest thanks to all of you for your encouragement through the writing of this book: Skip and Jennifer, Scott and Christy, Steve and Heather, and all my students.

Dedication

This book is dedicated to my very special granddaughters Megan, Paige, Peyton, Maddie and Kennedy (and grandchildren yet to arrive), all of whom I fully expect to become extraordinary influences in their students' lives thanks to the techniques of this book and those they are inspired to create as a result.

Additionally, I dedicate this book to Mr. Walter Bollinger, my eighth grade teacher at Lincoln Grade School in Nickerson, Kansas, without whose loving care, understanding and encouragement this book would not have materialized.

Although he left us many years ago, I can assure the readers of this book that Mr. Bollinger's loving influence still lingers in the hearts and minds of all he touched. I am me to a large part because of him. Thank you, Mr. Bollinger.

Introduction

I am thrilled to share my world of excitement, love, enthusiasm and adventure with you. It's a world where new and old ideas excite us each and every day. A world where my students have learned two sayings: "It's my time" (to teach and your time to learn) and "Yes, I can."

In my teaching days, when students had difficulty memorizing my 68-item timeline or other important dates, names or events, I'd tell them to say, "YES, I CAN." I did not accept the student's response, "I can't do it," because I believe that you get what you demand from your students and yourself.

Stan Cody

I've had the pleasure of teaching children in grades one through twelve. That experience taught me that children learn best when they understand why and how. Why was there a Boston Tea Party? How did Washington and his troops survive winter cold and snow at Valley Forge?

My students succeeded in part because of the demonstrations of events in our classroom. Why did this work so well? Because children love movies, television and pictures in books. They enjoy acting out history lessons in character costumes. It gives them visual references to memorize. They not only connect with the topic visually, mentally and emotionally, they also learn it forever. They relate dates, names and places to events that occur in today's world from conversations and world events to movies, and they understand the events that precipitated today's happenings and the history behind them.

Today's special challenges

Books don't always tell the whole truth. Later developments sometimes introduce insight that rightfully changes what was previously believed and written as the truth. In class, I emulated contemporary radio legend Paul Harvey with his "The Rest of the Story." The little-known facts sometimes bring an event to life for students, such as how Andrew Jackson cheated in his famous duel in which he killed a man and how Edwin Booth saved the life of President Lincoln's son, Robert Todd Lincoln, years before Booth's brother, John Wilkes Booth, assassinated Robert Todd Lincoln's father. Anecdotes like these add importance. They make history live and they make it fun. After teaching a history lesson, my students began to ask, "What's the rest of the story?" Wouldn't it be fun to know the "rest of the story" about everything?

Teachers are challenged to keep the students interested in learning. I kept my students excited about coming to my class by building suspense about what teaching method would be used each day. Once you realize you're an actor on a stage and you begin to introduce fun and excitement, students want to be sitting in your classroom, not another. Every day is a new adventure!

My students never knew which of my seventeen methods I'd introduce in the classroom on a particular day, which is to say that every day was fresh and new. They were expectant, anticipating the fun. Together, we learned through audio story tapes, singing historical songs (with me playing my banjo, of course), acronyms, palindromes, contests, story-telling, jokes, costumed characters (with me acting the part), and more.

Fellow teachers dubbed my classroom "The Museum," because it truly looked like one! In it were displayed early American tools, costumes and everyday objects of use (from the 1600s to the late 1800s). Think of a TGI Friday's® with all the memorabilia hanging on the restaurant walls. Each item demonstrated a slice of life in an era of American history. The "museum" included whaling and musketry utensils and tools, animal trapping equipment, letters written by Horace Greeley, Civil War bonds and 1862 newspapers displaying reports of Civil War battles.

But there's more to learning than simply hanging a musket or a bear trap on the wall. Students must be involved. There has to be a connection with the event, place or person in order for the learning experience to occur. We created the connection through experience: Students participated in churning butter, making cider, sauerkraut, candles, dandelion pizza, rattlesnake stew, pig sausage. We cooked with buffalo dung and preserved foods without refrigeration, including eggs and meat (which I ate in front of the class later in the year, proving our preservation methods worked).

Costumes! I loved dressing in character costumes of historical eras – and my students enjoyed my impersonations and learned from them. Johnny Appleseed visited our classroom, as did Davy Crockett, the pilgrim William

Brewster, General Cornwallis, Susan B. Anthony and the poor Chinese coolie that worked on the railroad.

While you may not want to use these same hands-on activities, I hope you carry on with the idea that children (and adults) learn from visual references and experience.

Advice for Success

Here's my advice: Be absurd. Do the unexpected. Do it repetitively.

When I was in college, I had a 63-year-old English professor, pretty and petite Miss Bender, who never spoke above a loud whisper. She devised a simple way to teach our class the differences in the words "to," "too" and "two."

"You all know that 'two' is the number and easy to remember and that 'to' is like a direction and therefore is a preposition. But that word 'too' is tricky."

She then told us that 'too' was her favorite because it had character. "Imagine," she said, "a lot of OOOOOOOOOOOOOOOOOOs coming out of my mouth in a straight line, one after the other, as I tell you this little story." And then she told the story that perfectly illustrated 'too:'

"I had been a good girl my whole life, but my brother was a real pain. He did everything wrong; I did everything right. You know – the perfect little girl who was always polite and helpful. Well, my brother had just thrown a temper tantrum. My mother said she was going to take him out to get some ice cream to settle him down and make him behave. I was not invited. As they left, I ran to the door and shouted that I wanted to go tooooooooooooooooo, meaning alsooooooooooo."

As my petite, quiet-spoken teacher ended her story, she stuck her head out the door and yelled "tooooooooooo" at the top of her lungs. It was completely out of character for her, but I never forgot the difference between 'to' and 'too.' She had come out of her box and, as a result, I learned.

What does it mean to be out of the box?

It simply means don't follow the standard pattern of teaching techniques. Step outside your comfort zone. Teach by doing the unexpected, by using a new method, by varying your approach from day-to-day, by being fresh. Be totally interested in connecting with your students. Use unexpected twists and turns and student participation methods to help them connect with the topic and learn. Liven up your class with new ideas, fun activities and creative methods that inspire your students and motivate and involve them in the learning process.

When students discover desire for learning and your teaching abilities accelerate, you discover the rewards that inspired you to become a teacher in the first place.

In this book, I'll share ideas to help you inject life into your classroom: ideas to help students learn and help you control your classroom while making school the easy, fun, interesting part of life it was meant to be.

The rewards are great!

I can tell you that the rewards for being an out-of-the-box teacher are great. Parents I've met on the street have exclaimed that my classes helped turn their children around, instilling confidence and improving their self-image. And, oh the joy, of being recognized at the local shopping mall when a former student hollers,

"Hey, Mr. Cody!" Or of being entered into a blog on the Internet as someone's favorite teacher. These little happenings thrill my soul. If I'd made a million dollars a day doing another job in life, I could not get as excited as when students come to me all bright and cheery to share the excitement of learning and ask, "What are we doing today, Mr. Cody?"

Teaching United States history is not just about a book or the political events that molded our great country. It is the life of everyday people and how they struggled to build a better life for themselves and posterity. My students deserved the best. Your students do, too. They deserve a teacher who connects them with learning, who teaches out of the box!

Stan's Axioms

- When teaching history, it is important for students to learn what has happened – and to know why it happened.

- Teaching and learning must be fun and they must be exciting.

- Nothing succeeds like constant success or fails like constant failure.

- Tenderness, love and a strong arm in directing are essentials for good teaching.

- Nothing is worth more to a child than feeling that he and his ideas are worthy, important, accepted and probably most of all, desired by others.

- Ridicule and sharp, cutting words are more destructive than any handicap this world can load on a student.

- Probably the most important thing a teacher can do, besides learning and using a student's name appropriately, is to PRAISE, PRAISE, PRAISE.

Teaching: An Engaging Occupation

Perhaps you remember teachers who made learning fun for you. They're the ones whose names and activities you remember with pleasure today! You felt you were actually capable of learning their material, and because of their ability to help you connect with the subject, you really did learn. They were the teachers who completely engaged your mind. You participated in the learning process enthusiastically.

On the other hand, you may recall teachers who ruled with an iron fist, who were dispassionate or uncaring, who removed the joy from learning or caused you to feel inadequate. They're the ones who taught material that seemed overwhelming or fraught with problems, and their classes are not especially the ones you want to remember today.

Teachers today must be on their toes and in touch with their students throughout each teaching hour. The teacher who is ineffective or unliked contributes to a difficult learning environment. This could be because the teacher:

- is bored
- is improperly or inadequately trained
- holds prejudice toward the subject
- holds prejudice toward the student
- is unhappy or in a poor frame of mind
- is self absorbed or pre-occupied
- never experienced a fun learning environment and has no role model or example of a fun teacher
- tends toward laziness and is not motivated to implement interesting, fun teaching methods
- is over-worked, stressed, burned out, tired or ill
- lacks interest in the students and their success
- believes the ability to create a fun learning environment requires assets he or she does not have, such as: *Creativity, props and visual aids, money, ability to act and to entertain, a lot of preparation time*

All these factors and beliefs impact our effectiveness as teachers. Teachers are really, really special and if they learn to work with and conquer their liabilities, they can make learning enjoyable and make a huge difference in the direction of their students' lives.

Teachers are not always to blame when students fail. After all, not all students' minds are fertile ground ripe for planting.

Stan Cody as Benjamin Franklin

Even excellent teachers using out-of-the-box teaching methods may be limited to some extent by their students' frame of mind or body. And there are a myriad of circumstances that block the path of learning. Students are affected by many outside and internal influences:

- The student's family and friends discourage, downplay or ridicule learning.

- No incentives are present. What's in it for them?

- The student is not praised when he/she does learn.

- Demonstrations of intelligence are laughed at by friends or family.

- The student suffers from low self-esteem and is belittled by others.

- The student's diet needs improvement. (It

may include high sugar and white flour content, resulting in a sugar "high" and a bad sugar "low;" or high salt content from all those French fries and packaged foods, resulting in lethargy.)

- The child is ill or in poor physical condition.
- The child is fatigued and needs sleep.
- The student does not like the teacher.
- The class or student lacks proper teaching materials.
- The room is too hot, too cold, smelly or uninteresting or not conducive to learning.
- The student is physically afraid of the teacher or other students.
- The learner is afraid of mental abuse from others.
- The learner is afraid while walking to and from school or the bus stop.
- The student is pre-occupied with thoughts of events, obligations, physical problems, people and circumstances outside the classroom or the school day.

There are other circumstances that affect a student's openness to learning, but the above list is a good start.

With undesirable home lives and the influences of television, music, movies, people, events and just "life," the challenge for kids to remain attentive in

class is sometimes overwhelming. That's why being "out of the box" is absolutely necessary for our
success as teachers and their success as students.
We must get their attention and engage their minds
in order to get their involvement, and the best way
to do that is to use positive, reinforcing, sometimes
absurd and always unique teaching techniques and
tools.

A teacher who can reach an otherwise unreach-
able, reluctant or difficult child is in a position to
transcend impossibilities. If you can generate a spark
of desire that leads to personal involvement, interest and learning, you can help the child take the first
step onto the path of academic success and achieve-
ment. An out-of-the-box teacher can help the student
move beyond his or her circumstances.

*Step out of your box!
Be bold! Try unique
and different teaching
techniques!*

Stan's Out-of-the-Box Stories

Yes, You Can Do This

I've been warned numerous times that I could not use a certain story or example in the classroom because the students wouldn't relate to it and wouldn't participate.

I just love when that happens because I like to turn the situation around and show that, yes, I can do that and, yes, my students do  connect and participate. Even the most polished of teachers have been surprised at this sort of success in the classroom.

Nobody knows everything about teaching. What works for one may not work for another. But don't be afraid to try. Don't hesitate to step out of the box and try something different, something uniquely colorful or imaginative, to connect with your students.

I must confess that there have actually been a handful of times when my great idea flopped. And that's fine. If more than three decades of teaching have only produced a few failures, I'm willing to swallow my pride with those odds and keep trying. ☑

For Learning to be Fun, Teaching Must be Fun

There's an old adage that says that in order to maintain proper teacher student respect, a teacher shouldn't smile before Thanksgiving or laugh before Christmas. Well, that's just plain wrong.

On my first day of school when I was in the fifth or sixth grade, I took one look at my science book and knew I was going to have fun. "Look at all these experiments!," I said to myself, practically jumping up and down for joy.

And then I scrolled through my new history book, and the great pictures of Indians, sailors and pilgrims spoke right to me.

I was in my element. Science and History were going to be fun this year!

Yep, and it took all of about three days, if that long, for my balloon to deflate itself. I quickly saw that it was going to be the same boring routine I'd had the year before. As soon as the teacher said, "Now turn to page seven in your textbook and we will start by having Billy read the first three paragraphs," the dye was cast.

Well, Billy, like many of us, was not a good reader. It would take Billy several minutes to stumble through the text. And then it would be another poor reader's turn to stumble while the rest of us struggled to follow along...or lost interest completely.

By the time the second reader started, not having understood any of the material, I'd made eye contact with Timmy, who was making funny faces at me. The hour dragged as student readers droned on. My chair was beginning to feel awfully hard on my bottom by the time the last student finished reading. And, guess what? It wasn't even Reading Class!

Then, of course, the teacher would end the class by saying, "Now, for your homework tonight, I want you to read the last three pages and answer the questions at the end of the chapter." We got nothing out of the first pages of the chapter and were expected to skip to the last three and do questions based on the whole chapter!

We've all suffered through these classroom nightmares. Did you like yours?

Of course, you didn't!

Stan Cody portrayed many historical characters in order to help his students connect visually with their lessons. The pioneer lady of the Old West was one.

Stan's Out-of-the-Box Stories

Teaching Can Be So Rewarding!

The other night while visiting my son, Steve, I noticed him playing around on his computer. I think he was participating in a blog at one point, and then he browsed around in a search engine. Out of curiosity, he typed in my name. The results included a posting by my former student, Megan Marshall.

Megan's message began with a saying that had helped my eighth graders, including Megan, remember the original thirteen colonies. Megan named the colonies and talked about how her U.S. history class changed her life: "It was the most exciting class I've ever been in," she said. Then she shared some of the fun things we did in class.

"He (my teacher) would wear clothes in

costume of the character we were learning about. I never realized it, but he used an unusual method to get the most (impact) out of each costume (and I am sure he knew what he was doing when he did it).

"The first day, he would wear the whole outfit and the next few days he would just wear part of the outfit. It always reminded me of the whole outfit and I got to wondering what part of the outfit he would wear each day. He knew it kept us on our toes and got us thinking. I think he had seventeen or eighteen outfits, but this way, he could wear an outfit for a full week with great results. That was always fun.

"Then there were the times we would preserve meat, eggs and carrots the way the pilgrims did, without refrigerators. Oh, my gosh, he even cooked the meat and eggs in the Spring of the year over an honest-to-goodness buffalo dung fire as the Oregon Trail people did.

"Then he would eat the preserved food to show us the methods really did work. But, no, he never let us eat any of the food except for the Dandelion Pizza, which we fixed like Johnny Appleseed did.

"I guess if I had to put it briefly, I would say, he just made it so much fun! Sometimes,

I would be sitting in a different teacher's classroom wondering, What is (Mr. Cody) going to do today?

"Basically (Yep, out-of-the-box), Mr. Cody taught out-of-the-box and I am sure he did that for his entire 33 years of teaching."

In closing, Megan said she always looked forward to her U.S. history class, because it was exciting to find out what witty, fun and far out thing Mr. Cody was planning to do that day. She ended by saying thanks to me and, of course, as my son was reading her words aloud, my heart went to my throat and a tear dripped onto my cheek. All I could say was, "I should still be teaching!" But my daughter-in-law, Heather, said, "No, Dad, you should be writing a program to help other teachers. That way you would reach perhaps thousands of students instead of 180 kids a year.☑

Connecting with Students through Fun Teaching Methods

Rhymes, Riddles & More

Although I knew what visiting parents and teachers' first question would be after observing my class, it always shocked me a little.

"Are your students always this quiet?"

I'd just smile and say, "Yep."

Why were the students so quiet and attentive? Because I was willing to be on stage every day in order to get their attention and involvement.

If you take that extra step that requires you to perform well on your classroom stage, it will pay off in results and admiration.

For example, in studying the Civil War, I knew that 1860s drill sergeants had a terrible time trying to teach their men to march. I explained to my students that most of the men did not know their left from their right, a basic concept that would help them learn to march in step and in unison as a group.

The Pilgrim leader William Proctor was a favorite characterization.

When the drill instructor said, "Your left, your left, your left; your right, left," invariably, the men fouled up.

But the soldiers, being farmers, knew the difference between hay and straw. So I did what the Civil War drill sergeants had learned to do. At a local tack and feed store, the clerk gave me a handful of hay and a handful of straw. In my class, I put hay in my left sock and straw in my right sock and repeated the order as the drill sergeants did. Instead of using the words "left" and "right," I said "hay foot" and "straw foot."

"Hay foot, hay foot; hay foot; straw foot; hay foot."

I still have my baggies of hay and straw. My students learned more than just the difference between hay and straw, however. They learned a small slice of life, the nitty gritty of military training, for Civil War recruits. They gained an appreciation for that war and every soldier who has ever trained for any war.

Method Ideas for Teaching

While studying and earning their credentials in college, teachers learn many teaching methods from other teachers and through continuing education. If you have experience with an effective method that does not appear in the following list of mnemonics, I'd love to hear from you. Just drop me a note at *stan@stancody.com*.

Perhaps you've tried these:

- Acronyms
- Acronymal sentences
- The absurd: Eat a worm (see story, end of chapter)
- Ridiculous examples
- Dramatic readings
- Games (See "Rappos" later in the book)
- Items of interest
- Jeopardy lights (Just like on the television game show)
- Let the kids figure it out
- Song parodies (Replace the words to a well-known song)
- Plays (from a book; or a student-written play)
- Preposition (sayings and the like)

- Poems (students write the poems)
- Play on words
- I stand on The Fifth (Amendment)
- Differences and contrasts between people, places, events
- Palindromes
- Picture puzzles
- Repetition
- Riddles
- Stories
- Spelling differences/endings (attic and sock)
- Songs (adjectives, nouns, pronouns)
- Similarities (native and foreign teen)
- Shoot shots for extra points
- Rhymes, letter series and number series (A B C D E F G - you and me; 1, 2, 3 - bad grades are after me)
- Earthworm (I left my heart in a 7-11® store) (See "More Fun" chapter)
- Stopwatch (time the Students versus the Determiners)
- Word associations (the bow of a ship, a bow tie, a pretty bow)
- Jokes

I've introduced you to a smorgasbord of ideas (above), most of which will not make sense until we talk about them in the pages to come. Just know that kids learn from association, visualization and fun.

Be off the wall. Be absurd. Be a kid. Be fun! Connect.

Stan's Out-of-the-Box Stories

Eating Worms

I once told each of my five classes that I would eat a worm in front of the class if they could keep up with everything on my two big lists: 1) The preambles to the Declaration of Independence and, 2) the 68-item presiden-

tial timeline, what caused each event in the timeline and how each one affected the next event. Guess what? I ate four worms!

The students loved it. They went nuts! I wore a bib and I cut up each worm into five pieces. (They were the big night crawlers.) I used catsup on one piece, butter on another, hot sauce and who knows what else. I had a big Diet Pepsi ready for a swig when I needed it.

You think my regular students did well on that one? Even the Resource Specialist Program (RSP) kids learned the lists. They wanted to see Mr. Cody to eat a worm!

I expected a lot, I gave a lot and, Yes, I loved every minute of it.

And, get this: The reason I was able to get this kind of learning out of my students was that they were having as much fun as I was.

I can't say it enough: Fun, fun, fun – for your students; and for you.

Whether your students are good readers is beside the point. If you make the lesson interesting, demonstrate it visually and involve every member of the class in the process of learning, you can inspire and motivate your students to learn. They will love it, and so will you! ☑

Teaching with Mnemonics and Memorics

The sheer volume of information we are expected to learn in today's world can be overwhelming. Young people are exposed to thousands of details every day through television, radio, families, friends, church, extracurricular sports, clubs and school. When we simplify the learning process with a time-line or mnemonics, we give them a powerful tool that cuts through the maze and helps them cement the most important information in their minds – in order – forever.

Repetition, mnemonics and the timeline concept make learning long lists of details easier.

What would I do as a math teacher, to help my students learn addition, subtraction and multiplication in a short period of time? Consider this simplistic plan: The first week, I'd teach addition and give an addition test. The next week, I'd teach subtraction and give a test that includes at least one addition problem. The third week, I'd teach multiplication and on the test, I'd include multiplication with at least one addition problem and one subtraction problem.

The Chinese coolie played a big part in the settling of our nation and the Gold Rush experience. Stan Cody enjoyed this classroom portrayal.

Repetition, one of the keys to learning, is demonstrated in this plan. If you include a little addition on the subtraction test, you reinforce what the student learned about addition (without taking away from his subtraction learning). And so forth.

I don't teach something for a test alone. I want students to continually have practice with the basic concepts and facts so they won't forget them.

Yes, it does take a little time to teach repetitively, but we are teaching for eternity, not just for a test. It's worth the extra effort we as teachers can contribute to help the student's lifelong learning.

Students come back many years later and tell me they still know when the match was invented, when Eli Whitney came up with the interchangeable musket parts and when Oberlin College opened its doors to women. There are 68 items on my History Timeline. My regular students learn them and so do my special education students, because the timeline is constructed in a way that makes it easy to remember.

Using Mnemonics with Repetition and the History Timeline

I used mnemonics to help students learn the History Timeline. By the end of the year, 98 percent of the students, on average, could repeat the timeline in front of the class without error. And the two percent who couldn't recite the timeline knew far more than most students in other history classes. Those who did not memorize the timeline often did not invest time into learning it. You'll always have a percent who are not motivated or are affected by external influences (see Chapter 1).

Mnemonics is a memory improvement technique involving visual imagery, sounds, rhyming or formula to trigger the memory of things, such as the order of events or names. Here's a rhyming example:

In 1492, Columbus sailed the ocean blue.

How You Can Put Mnemonics to Work in Your Classroom

Let me share a thought about memory techniques. Most people call them mnemonics, but in real, everyday terms, I like to use the word that I coined: Memorics.

You've probably seen several excellent demonstrations of memory specialists on television. There are many types of memory saving techniques and I think I can safely say that a single one of them will not be sufficient as a memory tool for all purposes. And they're not effective for everyone.

If a certain mnemonic or memoric helps your students learn, it's right. When using memory techniques, the key is enthusiasm. If you are absolutely convinced and sold on the activity and you can transfer your excitement to your students, your students will be 100 percent participatory.

I should mention that the more your students trust you and like you, the easier it will be for them to catch your enthusiasm and grab hold of the methods you so strongly believe in.

There's a Secret to Mnemonic Success!

Here's an inside tip for teaching mnemonics that I know has contributed to the success of my students: You must know and let the children know that if they make the mnemonic, it becomes theirs. They will remember the material much more easily and retain it longer, if they created it.

I remember when my class made up the mnemonic for the Cycle of Life song. I wrote on the board the one I had come up with; and then I asked them to replace words or phrases with their own. Each student had an opportunity to share his or her idea with the whole class.

What we ended up with was not mine (except for minor parts). The new song came from Tony, some from Gina and Jasmine, and one word from Harley.

This sort of exercise calls upon skills in a little different manner than most lessons and uses talents other lessons don't. Some of your C and D students, or even failing students, will come up with the best ideas. The point is that, if the students can put their name to it, it's theirs and it awards them recognition they desire and deserve.

Stan's Examples of Mnemonics and *Memorics*

Here's a partial list of mnemonics and memorics I've used successfully. You'll find others in the later pages and lesson plans of this book. You can use these as they are or use them as starting points to create your own (or have your students create their own):

Acronyms

SCUBA – Self Contained Underwater Breathing Apparatus

FACE – The spaces between the notes on the scale

IOU - I owe you

Acronymal or mnemonic sentences

"Every Good Boy Does Fine (or Deserves Fudge)" illustrates an acronymal sentence that has helped millions of children learn the notes of the treble scale (EGBDF).

Pictures

The well-known character, Uncle Sam, dressed in the colors, stars and stripes of the American flag, has been used extensively to represent United States politics and calls to serve or contribute to national causes.

Word pictures

Using a cartoon or illustration with key words placed in key areas is helpful for simple concepts. Example: *Columbus discovered the Americas in 1492.*

Songs

A noun's a person, place or thing, a person, place or thing. (Tune: "Auld Lang Syne")

Poems and rhymes

Little Miss Muffet sat on her tuffet eating her goober peas. (Goober peas, or peanuts, were a favorite snack among Confederate soldiers.) *Along came a Rebel and sat at the table and gave all her peas away.*

This one is a bit on the crude side, but kids love it, and it gets the point across quickly: Mary had a little lamb; the Yankee shot it dead; now Mary takes the lamb to school, between two hunks of bread.

Learning numbers in numerical order

1, 2, 3 – bad grades are after me.

Learning events in proper order with alphabet tricks

"B" comes before "S" – a "ball" comes before a "strike".

"Balls" are called first by the umpire.

Alphabet soup that ought to be tossed

I'm going to throw this in only because it's a good example of what *not* to use. It's more complex than simple and will serve only to confuse students. This good <u>bad example</u> makes use of rhyming to learn the alphabet:

ABCDEFG = *There are good grades for you and me.*

HIJKLMN = *The marines have a few good men.*

OPQRSTU = *We have food for our whole crew.*

Next VW = *I will promise you.*

XYZ = *Good friends for you and me.*

Bottom line tip

As you can see, memory techniques can integrate two or more types of devices. For example, with the aid of a word or two, a drawing may trigger the memory. My best advice when it comes to creating a mnemonic is to be free with your thinking. Let it flow. Not every idea is good and perhaps only one out of ten to fifteen will be useful or fantastic. But if you allow yourself to think freely and not be judgmental or self critical to the extent of hurting your credibility, you'll come up with some fun, memorable mnemonics to help your students learn and retain material easily.

Privacy note

Some students may create mnemonics they do not wish to share. The words, phrases, acronyms, etc. that they employ to help themselves remember may relate to a personal or family situation. That's OK. There are no rules and mnemonics can be privately owned. The test is whether the technique works for the student.

Sharing with the class

Children are free thinkers and that's wonderful; but sometimes their creativity can get them (and you) into trouble. Before you let students share with the class, ask them to show you their personally created mnemonics and acronyms. You get to review them first, to make sure they are acceptable and won't cause embarrassment or conflict with the student's parents or the school office.

Help! I need a mnemonic!

For some time, I have been trying to create a mnemonic, rhyme, acronym or memoric that will help students remember the twenty-sixth amendment. This amendment makes it legal for eighteen-year-olds to vote. I've thought on this many times, and it stumps me. If you think of a catchy memory technique for Amendment 26, please let me know by email me at *stan@stancody. com*. I'll give you the credit on my website at *www.stancody.com*.

Stan Cody welcomes your feedback, ideas and experiences using mnemonics and other memorics.

Stan's Out-of-the-Box Stories

Scott's Echo Room:
Challenging the Reluctant Student

Many times, I met students at the door as they arrived, shook their hands, called them by name and said, "Good morning," as they entered my classroom, which I called, "Scott's Echo Room."

Scott was a tall, handsome young man who had been held back in the eighth grade, and rightfully so, because he had failed every class except music in his first attempts. Scott's parents, although loving, did not understand parenting or teaching, and I doubt that praise occupied a place in their vocabulary.

Scott was unaware that he was bright. He believed he could not learn. His mother had told him many times, "I don't know what to do with you. You are smart. Don't you want to learn? It's important, it's important, it's important."

I can hear her so clearly, just telling her son to learn but not showing him or helping him to learn.

Perhaps if you understand that Scott was

a fantastic, highly talented drummer and that the Jazz Band in which he played had won many national awards, and that another competition loomed on the horizon, you'll know how sharp Scott's intellect was.

I did not have the opportunity to teach Scott in his first year or throughout the first trimester of his second attempt at eighth grade. He had not had the pleasure of out-of-the-box teaching, and he was receiving all "Fs." He transferred into my class on the guarantee from him to me, that he would learn the 1996 timeline of 68 events, learn the presidents in proper order and write the papers I required. He accepted these requirements because he had heard from my other students that he'd have fun and want to learn and that he would learn.

I gave Scott a proper amount of time to catch up with the class and I kept a close eye on his progress. Of course, he knew that even if he failed all courses again, because of his large size and his age, he would be promoted. He also knew that if he did not learn and meet requirements, he could not participate in the love of his life: Music – at least not as he wanted to.

The other teachers had given in and signed permission slips to let Scott attend music events. Even the principal was going to let him attend the upcoming band competition because he felt music was the only thing Scott had going for him and he shouldn't be discouraged from participating. The music director had said that Scott was so good that, without him, the band might as well not compete.

Actions of the other teachers and principal actually helped me as I became the culprit who said, "No, you can't go until you learn your timeline." It didn't make Scott very happy, but it was my requirement. I stuck to my guns and, guess what? Scott learned his timeline in two days. It was not an easy task, but he did it! He had a great incentive – playing with the band – that had never been present before.

The next time a contest came along, Scott didn't tell me until the day of the event, expecting me to cave in and let him go. He had not memorized the presidents. I just said, "Sorry, learn them." At 4:30 that afternoon, he repeated all 42 of the presidents in order and I signed his permission slip so he could go to the contest that evening. The band competed and won!

I called my classroom Scott's Echo Room because Scott successfully repeated the lesson beyond his own expectations and his success was echoed in his being able to attend the competition. This story taught Scott about life.

Post Script

Scott made a special request of me: "Whenever you see me or when I come into your classroom, say, 'Yes, I can.'" I did, he did and his grades kept improving. He began to feel good about himself. I saw him just the other day and his grades in high school were all passing.

Ah, our successes as teachers may seem small, but are they not wonderful?

***

The above story relates to the familiar tale of the little boy who visited the Grand Canyon with his parents and discovered his ability to shout and hear his voice return in an echo. Instead of shouting, as he did initially, "Hey!," "Shut up!" and "I hate you!," he finally took Mom's advice and belted out, "I love you!" What came back was pretty much what he sent out. ☑

United States History Timeline

Over the years, my mnemonic history timeline has endeared itself to the hearts and minds of hundreds of my students. Many of them will freely tell you that the Townshend Act was enacted in 1767; they recall quite well that the Battle of Bunker Hill occurred in 1775; and "washtubs" still helps them attach Washington and his Valley Forge troops with the year 1777-1778.

By learning the mnemonic sentences throughout the year, your students will learn the 68-item timeline of U.S. history and the cause and effect of each event in the timeline. Each week, they write the sentences, the related events (according to the time-table) and the presidents (in chronological order).

On testing the timeline, grading is as follows:

- Miss any part of the Timeline sentences, student receives a 0 (3 possible)

- Miss any of the events, receive a 0 (5 possible)

- Miss any of the presidents, receive 0 (3 possible)

I always stayed late after school on Wednesdays to keep current with grades and plans. If the students wanted to stay after school for 40 minutes to work on the timeline, I gave them a credit grade with no points for that week's grade. It only helped with their grade point, which is what counted, as they did not receive an F grade. (If a student failed the test but came in on Wednesday and studied for 40 minutes, the student received an "E" for "excused," which did not impact the final grade.)

History Timeline Trivia

You'll notice that on the timeline that follows, all dates that end in a "1" deal with freedoms: 1681 William Penn's free worship; 1781, America was free from British control; 1791, the Bill of Rights; 1821, the first free public schools in America; 1831, Nat Turner's slave revolt to freedom; and 1861, President Lincoln freed the slaves.

Feel free to use my U.S. History Timeline and make copies for your students. In fact, I always kept a box of timeline copies my students could (and did) pick up weekly. You can download my timeline in PDF form at *www.StanCody.com*.

The mnemonic sentences below are listed and graded each week. As you'll see in the timeline on the following pages, I used them to relate to the historical events. Notice that the first letter of each important word is capitalized, because the first letter represents a keyword which begins with the same letter and helps to recall a specific event. Any word not capitalized is used only to help make a sentence.

1. My Crying Robot, JT, Found Wives Compacting Pilgrim Harvard With Slow Acid.

2. Georgiana French Proclaimed Townshend Massacred Partygoers Including: Daniel-Boone, Lex-Concord and Bunker-Hill in Washtubs.

3. Corny Wallace Said 3/5 Accepted Washington's Patent Office Rights.

4. Eli Whitney's Muskets Purchased Lewis Matches.

5. Steaming With Burning Banners, Opra Missed School.

6. Meanwhile, Erie Started T-Thumb's Church Shooting Revolvers.

7. Never Battling Morse, O'Trail Smith Fought

Howie Young, Giving Lincoln Civil-War,
Freed Slaves, Widows, Death, Railroads And
Outlaws.

About the Mnemonic U.S. History Timeline

The timeline (later in this chapter) that helped my
students learn the highlights and important events
in American history became a popular tool over
the years. Former students still refer to "Mr. Cody's
Timeline," recognizing how the timeline's acronymal
statements helped them to learn a myriad of names,
places and dates.

The names of all United States presidents appear
in the right-side column of the Timeline. They are
not intended to correspond chronologically with the
historical events or dates noted in the columns to
their left.

You'll notice I've scheduled "tests" throughout the
timeline. While the testing dates are displayed for the
purpose of example, I do strongly suggest that each
test cover the new material just learned AND the
material covered in previous sessions and tests.

Comments? I'd love to hear your feedback and
your questions. Just drop me a note at *stan@stan-
cody.com.*

U.S. History Timeline

(Note: Presidents do not correspond with dates or events represented by the acronymal sentences to their left.)

1. My Crying Robot JT Found Wives Compacting Pilgrim Harvard With Slow Acid

Mnemonic	Year	Event	President
My	1215	Magna Carta	Washington
Crying	1492	Columbus discovered the Americas	Adams
Robot	1587	Roanoke Island	Jefferson
JT	1607	Jamestown founded	
Found	1619	First blacks in America	
Wives	1619	Wives for sale in Jamestown	
			Test 1; September 10
Compacting	1620	Mayflower compact	Madison
Pilgrim	1620	Pilgrims at Plymouth	
Harvard	1636	Harvard University	Monroe
With	1681	William Penn (Pennsylvania)	
			Test 2; September 18
Slow	1692	Salem witch hunt	J.Q. Adams
Acid	1732	Poor Richard's Almanac	Jackson
			Test 3; September 25

2. Georgiana French Proclaimed Townshend Massacred Partygoers Including Daniel Boone, Lex Concord and Bunker Hill In Washtubs

Mnemonic	Year	Event	President
Georgiana	1733	Georgia Colony founded	Van Buren
French	1756	French and Indian War (7-Year War)	W.H. Harrison
			Test 4; October 2
Proclaimed	1763	Proclamation of '63	Tyler
Townshend	1767	Townshend Acts	Polk
			Test 5; October 12
Massacred	1770	Boston, Massachusetts	Taylor
Partygoers	1773	Boston Tea Party	Filmore
Including	1774	Intolerable Acts	Pierce
			Test 6; October 16
Daniel Boone	1775	Boone to Kentucky	Buchanan
Lex Concord	1775	Lexington–Concord	Lincoln
and Bunker Hill	1775	Battle of Bunker Hill	
			Test 7; October 23
In	1776	Declaration of Independence	A. Johnson
Washtubs	1777-78	Washington and Troops at Valley Forge	Grant
			Test 8; October 30

3. Corny Wallace Said 3/5 Accepted Washington Patent Office Rights

Mnemonic	Year	Event	President
Corny Wallace	1781	Cornwallis surrenders at Yorktown	
Said	1786	Shay's Rebellion	Hayes
			Test 9; November 6
3/5	1787	3/5 Compromise	Garfield
Accepted	1788	U.S. Constitution passed	Arthur
Washington	1789	Washington becomes first U.S. president	Cleveland
			Test 11; November 20
Patent Office	1790	U.S. Patent Office opens	Harrison
Rights	1791	Bill of Rights passed	
			Test 12; December 4

4. Eli Whitney's Muskets Purchased Lewis Matches

Mnemonic	Year	Event	President
Eli	1793	Eli Whitney introduces the cotton gin	Cleveland
			Test 13; December 11
Whitney's	1794	Whiskey Rebellion	McKinley
Muskets	1798	Eli Whitney's musket parts	
Purchased	1803	Louisiana Purchase (France, Jefferson, Napoleon)	
Lewis	1804	Lewis and Clark explore Pacific Northwest	
			Test 14; December 18
Matches	1805	First matches invented	T.R. Roosevelt

5. Steaming With Burning Banners, Opra Missed School

Mnemonic	Year	Event	President
Steaming	1807	Fulton's steamboat (Cleremont)	Taft
			Test 15; January 8
With	1812	War with England (War of 1812)	Wilson
Burning	1814	British burn Washington, D.C.	Harding
Banners	1814	Francis Scott Key writes "The Star Spangled Banner"	Coolidge
			Test 16; January 15
Opra	1818	National Road opens	Hoover
Missed	1820	Missouri Compromise	F.D. Roosevelt
			Test 17; January 29
School	1821	First free public school (I 8 A #2 pencil in school)	Truman

6. Meanwhile, Erie Started T-Thumb's Church Shooting Revolvers

Mnemonic	Year	Event	President
Meanwhile	1823	Monroe Doctrine	Eisenhower
			Test 18; February 5
Erie	1825	Erie Cnal opens (25 cents to ride)	Kennedy
Started	1828	Approximate start of the Trail of Tears	L. Johnson
			Test 19; February 12
T.Thumb's	1830	Tom Thumb's train runs	Nixon
Church	1830	Mormon Church started by Joseph Smith	Ford
			Test 20; February 26
Shooting	1831	Nat Turner's Slave Rebellion	Carter
Revolvers	1833	Sam Colt's revolver pistol (3 + 3 = 6 shooter)	Reagan
			Test 21; March 5

7. Never Battling Morse, O'Trail Smith Fought Howie Young Giving Lincoln Civil War, Freed Slaves, Widows, Death, Railroads And Outlaws

Mnemonic	Year	Event	President
Never	1835	Narcissa to Oregon (missionary)	GHW Bush
Battling	1836	Battle of the Alamo	
			Test 22; March 19
Morse	1844	Samuel Morse telegraph	Clinton
O'Trail	1844	Approximate start of the Oregon Trail	
Smith	1844	Mormon leader Joseph Smith killed (lynch mob); was presidential candidate	
			Test 23; March 26
Fought	1845	U.S.-Mexican War	GW Bush
Howie	1846	Elias Howe sewing machine	
Young	1847	Young and Mormons to Utah	
Giving	1849	California Gold Rush begins	
Lincoln	1861	Abraham Lincoln president	
Civil War	1861	Civil War begins	
			Test 24; April 2
Freed Slaves	1863	Emancipation proclamation freed certain slaves	
			Test 25; April 9
Widows	1865	Civil War ends	
Death	1865	John Wilkes Booth kills President Lincoln	
Railroads	1869	Transcontinental Railroad completed	
			Test 26; April 23
And	1872	Susan B. Anthony arrested for voting	
Outlaws	1882	Outlaw Jesse James killed	

Note: After this date, tests are given weekly. Sometimes all the Timeline dates are tested; sometimes half.

Stan's Out-of-the-Box Stories

The Box Lunch Social

One year while teaching United States history, I demonstrated an old-fashioned nineteenth century American social custom. I asked the girl students to make picnic baskets to be auctioned off to the highest bidders. I explained that each boy would pay up to three dollars to eat with the maker of the basket he bought. He would dance the first dance of the evening with her.

Five classes and 135 students participated. (Money we collected was used to pay a professional square dance caller for the dance  activity after the meal.) The names of the creators of the picnic baskets were secret; some girls even carried the baskets of their friends to fool the boys.

But wait a minute. I'm getting ahead of my story.

Even before we started the activity, the principal at the time (a lady) and the past principal (a man) called me to the office. They advised me that they thought the activity might give the appearance of being sexist and cause some repercussions among parents. So I asked their advice.

The former principal suggested I ask half the boys to bring baskets along with half the girls. Explain to the students that this isn't really the way our ancestors conducted their picnic basket auctions. He was sure the students would understand.

It got a little quiet in the principal's office as I considered this suggestion. Then, quietly, I said, "That's just great. Why didn't I think of that? And when it comes time for the study of the Civil War, since I am from the South, I'll teach them that the South won (silence)."

It got even quieter in that office. The two principals looked at each other.

"Well, what's the difference?," I asked.

They finally said I could try the picnic social exercise this year and that we'd evaluate the program for next year.

You know, we did it the right way the next year, too. ☑

Foundations of Freedom

The U.S. Constitution, Bill of Rights & Preamble

The Preamble to the Constitution

The Preamble to our Constitution makes a statement on behalf of the citizens of the United States, offering a bird's eye view to the rights and freedoms enjoyed by all our country's citizens:

We the people of the United States, in order to form a more perfect union, establish justice, insure domestic tranquility, provide for the common defense, promote the general welfare, and secure the blessings of liberty to ourselves and our posterity, do ordain and establish this constitution for the United States of America.

The Preamble is fairly easy to teach and easy for students to learn:

We the people of the United States

The citizens of our country, our 50 states.

In order to form a more perfect union

We know that all governments are troubled with problems of certain groups of people trying to impose their will on others. We will try to make our government as perfect and fair as possible.

Establish justice

Set up a government that is fair for everybody as much as this is possible.

Insure domestic tranquility

Make life here in the United States as peaceful and safe as possible.

Provide for the common defense

Secure our country from outside interference which may try to impose their desires on our country by making us their slaves.

And secure the blessings of liberty

Assure that the blessing of freedom is maintained for all our citizens.

To ourselves and our posterity

All the things we assure for ourselves we also want to assure for our children and those who follow them.

Do ordain and establish

Make this document and its assurances official.

This constitution for the United States of America.

The rules and regulations for our country.

Amendments to the Constitution

Some 27 amendments have been made to the United States Constitution since the Constitution was passed in 1788. *Note: The first ten amendments are known as the Bill of Rights.* Learning the highlights and the amendments that impact us most directly can be challenging to students whose school days and homework assignments are filled with numbers, dates and names.

So, here are some suggestions for teaching the amendments. Use them as they are or improve upon them (and feel free to email me about what works best for you). Note that I've included a QUIZ for the Bill of the Rights (the first ten amendments, indicated with underlining) and an EXAM for all the amendments, at the end of the chapter.)

Amendment #1: The first amendment promises freedom of religion, assembly, petition, press, opinion and speech. Mnemonically, RAPPOS.

Amendment #2: I have the right **2** bear arms, not to arm bears. Notice the 2 is bold, big, underlined and displayed as a numeral, indicating the Second Amendment. The second amendment also approves a well-formed militia.

Amendment #3: No Housing Troops. There are three words in this mnemonic, representing the Third Amendment. The amendment says we do not have to house our military troops in peacetime, but we may. War time is a different matter: We may not have a choice. (This referred to the British Quartering Act.)

Amendment #4: What are you looking FOR? The Fourth Amendment says you need a search warrant to search my home or place of business. It's called the Search and Seizure Amendment and it is in reference to the Writ of Assistance.

Amendment #5: I am standing on the FIFTH. The Fifth Amendment says that I do not have to answer questions because, although I am innocent, answering may make me appear to be guilty. Another part of the Fifth Amendment deals with the "no double jeopardy" law. Once I have been tried and a Not Guilty verdict has been handed down, I cannot be tried again for the same crime in criminal court, even if I admit doing it. (See my Standing on the Fifth story at the end of this chapter.)

Amendment #6: Remember: public and speedy…trial. There are six letters in each of the words/phrases in parentheses, indicating this is the Sixth Amendment. It entitles us to a fair, public and speedy trial.

Amendment #7: Lucky 7. The lucky number in a game of craps (and on many slot machines) is the number seven. The Seventh Amendment makes us lucky because it ensures us a jury trial. It has been proven that the more people you have deciding a case, the better the chance you have of getting a correct verdict.

Amendment #8: Fair bail, fair fine, fair punishment. The Eighth Amendment promises us fair bail, a fair fine and fair punishment. "Fair bail" and "fair fine" each have eight letters. Or use "My horse **8** a **bail** of hay."

Amendment #9: Pick your nose amendment. It means that if it is not prohibited by the Constitution, then you can do it, i.e., pick your nose, brush your teeth, sing a song, drive a car, get married, dig a ditch, work as a butcher, break your own window, etc.

Amendment #10: The ten-sided stop sign amendment. It states that if the federal government does not want to set a rule for certain things and if it is not against the U.S. Constitution, the state has the right to set the rule. Of course, we have eight-sided stop signs, but we could have ten and call this the ten-sided Stop Sign amendment. The number of letters in the words, state rights, is ten, which can aid in remembering the amendment.

Note: The quiz for amendments 1-10 (the Bill of Rights) follows the twenty-seventh amendment.

Amendment #11: One person can't sue one state which is not his own state in federal court. A California resident cannot sue the state of Kansas (or any other state) without that state court's permission. (The two occurrences of the word "one" are the mnemonic: A "one" next to a "one" makes the number 11.)

Amendment #12: This amendment deals with the way we once elected our president. It is no longer in use.

Amendment #13: Lucky 13. This amendment freed the slaves. Think of the lucky thirteen colonies who freed themselves from British rule.

Amendment #14: Foreignteen-born and native-born have the same rights. "Foreignteen," my unique way of spelling "fourteen," was easily remembered for this amendment's promise that the same rights and protection of the law would be guaranteed to both foreign-born and native-born American citizens.

Amendment #15: Xv. The Fifteenth Amendment let all adult males vote, i.e., ex-slaves, etc. Many could not read or write so they entered an "X" for voting and their initial at the bottom of the ballet. Using an imaginary historical character named Victor, I taught this amendment with an "X" for voting and a "V" for Victor, which also gave us the "XV" in Roman Numerals for the number 15.

Amendment #16: Sixteen years of age. In today's world, a person may work without his parents' consent at age sixteen, but he must pay income tax. The Sixteenth Amendment lets the U.S. government collect tax on a person's income.

Amendment #17: Seventeen silly senators sat sleepily sipping sodas. Yes, I know this is silly, but sometimes silly things work. The Seventeenth

Amendment deals with the replacing of a Senator when one dies or is removed from office.

Amendment #18: Can you legally buy liquor at age 18? No. This amendment states that no one may sell, make or transport liquor. It is known as the Prohibition Amendment.

Amendment #19: Nineteen ladies went out to vote. Women finally got the right to vote with the Nineteenth Amendment in the year 1919. The first election in which they voted occurred in 1920.

Amendment #20: President takes over. The president takes office on January 20. Need I say more?

Amendment #21: Can you buy liquor at age 21? Sure. The Twenty-first Amendment repealed the Eighteenth (Prohibition) Amendment and once again allowed the making, selling and transporting of liquor.

Amendment #22: The president is limited to two terms in office. (2-2)

"It was always an honor to represent Uncle Sam to my students," says Stan.

Amendment #23: Disagree (or agree) in DC (rhymes with 23). The Twenty-third Amendment let the residents of Washington, DC vote in the presidential election.

Amendment #24: Where is the busiest place on Earth on December 24? Of course, the North Pole. I shortened it to No Pol, meaning no poll tax for voting. The Twenty-fourth Amendment says you cannot charge a person to register to vote.

Amendment #25: Twenty-fifth president (McKinley) killed in office. The Twenty-fifth Amendment tells us how to replace a president, living or dead.

Amendment #26: The Twenty-sixth Amendment lowered the voting age to eighteen years. You could introduce this as a math problem, since 26 eighteenths is somewhat of an improper fraction. Twenty-six is the amendment and eighteen is the voting age. It was *improper* to send troops to war without giving them the right to vote.

Amendment #27: Highest amendment number = highest salary. The Twenty-seventh Amendment tells us when a Congressman can get a pay raise.

Testing

The quiz that follows tests the students on their knowledge of the first ten amendments to the U.S. Constitution, or the Bill of Rights. It is, like the general amendments exam that follows it, based on my system of acronyms and mnemonics.

Bill of Rights Quiz

Place the correct amendment number next to the reference. The answers are shown below.

Score Total Correct: _____

Scoring Guide:
A = 18 - 20   B = 16 - 17
C = 14 - 15   D = 12 - 13

#	Clue	Amendment #
1	speech	____
2	no double jeopardy	____
3	no housing troops in peacetime	____
4	if the Federal government doesn't want it, the state can have it	____
5	assembly	____
6	fair trial	____
7	right to have a gun	____
8	form a militia	____
9	petition	____
10	brush your hair, marry, take a walk	____
11	search and seisure	____
12	opinion	____
13	standing on the fifth	____
14	public trial	____
15	press	____
16	bail	____
17	jury trial	____
18	fair punishment	____
19	fine	____
20	petition	____

Answers: 1-1; 2-5; 3-3; 4-10; 5-1; 6-6; 7-2; 8-2; 9-1; 10-9; 11-4; 12-1; 13-5; 14-6; 15-1; 16-8; 17-1; 18-8; 19-8; 20-1

Amendments to the Constitution Exam
Some questions are repeated intentionally. (Repetition is good!)

#	Clue	Amendment #
1	Guns	____
2	Income tax	____
3	No slavery	____
4	Sign a paper to support a cause	____
5	Petition	____
6	Native and foreign born have the same rights	____
7	President two terms in office	____
8	President is crazy	____
9	Self incrimination	____
10	Limits terms of presidents	____
11	No unusual punishments	____
12	Chinese can vote	____
13	Can't charge me to vote	____
14	I can make alcohol	____
15	Income tax	____
16	Way to replace a president	____
17	Repealed the eighteenth amendment	____
18	Freed the slaves	____
19	Fair bail	____
20	Replace a senator	____
21	No selling alcohol	____
22	President has two terms in office	____
23	You can sell alcohol	____
24	Assembly	____
25	Fair trial	____
26	Have an open public trial	____
27	I don't believe in God	____
28	Form a small, well organized military force	____
29	Repealed by the twenty-first amendment	____
30	Pray to a statue	____
31	A person from Iowa may not sue the state of Kansas in federal court	____

32	Eighteen-year-olds can vote	____
33	Let women vote	____
34	Press	____
35	Search warrant	____
36	When the president takes office	____
37	When the president can't do his job	____
38	California can turn right on a red light	____
39	I don't think the president is good	____
40	Replace a senator	____
41	You can't make me your slave	____
42	Can't stop me from voting because of previous servitude	____
43	No double jeopardy	____
44	When Congress gets a pay raise	____
45	Public trial	____
46	You can brush your teeth	____
47	Women's suffrage	____
48	Fair fine	____
49	Blacks can vote	____
50	Religion	____
51	Federal government doesn't want it, the state can have it	____
52	No alcohol	____
53	No slaves	____
54	Militia	____
55	Right to have a weapon	____
56	Speedy trial	____
57	January 20	____
58	Quartering Act	____
59	Writ of assistance	____
60	No transporting alcohol	____
61	If Constitution does not restrict it, you can do it	____
62	State can have it if Feds don't want it	____
63	No housing troops	____
64	When Congress gets a pay raise	____
65	Old way of electing a president	____
66	Can't charge me money to vote	____

67 No poll tax   ____
68 People in Washington, D.C.
    can vote for president   ____
69 Self incrimination   ____
70 Right to meet to talk
    about a problem   ____
71 No money charged to
    register to vote   ____
72 Opinion   ____
73 No making alcohol   ____
74 Public trial   ____
75 I can transport alcohol   ____
76 Jury trial   ____
77 Ex-slaves can vote   ____
78 Fair bail   ____
79 Speech   ____

Answers to the general amendments exam

1:	2	21:	18	41:	13	61:	9
2:	16	22:	22	42:	15	62:	10
3:	13	23:	21	43:	5	63:	3
4:	1	24:	1	44:	27	64:	27
5:	1	25:	6	45:	6	65:	12
6:	14	26:	6	46:	9	66:	24
7:	22	27:	1	47:	19	67:	24
8:	25	28:	2	48:	8	68:	23
9:	5	29:	18	49:	15	69:	5
10:	22	30:	1	50:	1	70:	1
11:	8	31:	11	51:	10	71:	24
12:	15	32:	26	52:	18	72:	1
13:	24	33:	19	53:	13	73:	18
14:	21	34:	1	54:	2	74:	6
15:	16	35:	5	55:	2	75:	21
16:	25	36:	20	56:	6	76:	7
17:	21	37:	25	57:	20	77:	15
18:	13	38:	10	58:	3	78:	8
19:	8	39:	1	59:	4	79:	1
20:	17	40:	17	60:	18		

Stan's Out-of-the-box Stories

Standing on the Fifth

Often when I speak to civic groups, I help the adult audience members learn the Fifth Amendment by using wordpictures and a demonstration. I stand on an empty whiskey bottle (a fifth of whiskey) and tell a little story that creates a visual image in the mind. I would not advise taking a whiskey bottle to class, but you might find an opportunity to use this example:

Tommy's parents left him alone overnight because he had been a responsible young man and they had a lot of trust in him. But no sooner had they gone than Tommy noticed his parents' liquor bar. Curiosity got the better of him, so he reached for the fifth of whiskey and took a sip. And then another sip. And then another, until he'd drunk a good portion.

Just then, the family car rolled back into the driveway. His mother ran into the room, saying she had forgotten her purse.

Now Tommy didn't want his mom to see the bottle, so, quickly, he laid it on the floor and stood on it.

His mother looked at him suspiciously and

asked, "Have you been into anything?"

Tommy replied rather sheepishly, "I'm standing on the fifth." ☑

Our Freedoms and Our Flag
Meet the Mnemonic, RAPPOS

The basic freedoms enjoyed by every American were won and earned for us through hard work, wars and the dedication and determination of those who set up our Constitution for posterity and peace.

I coined a new "word," RAPPOS. Yes, sometimes a weirdly spelled word helps the learning process! RAPPOS is a good start at teaching students the six fundamental freedoms every American citizen enjoys through the First Amendment to the United States Constitution:

The fundamental (RAPPOS) freedoms:

R = religion
A = assembly
P = petition
P = press
O = opinion
S = speech

Stan's Out-of-the-Box Stories

The World Turned Upside Down

My students loved the words to the song, "The World Turned Upside Down," reportedly played by the British, the world's most potent military power, upon their General Cornwallis's surrender to the French and Americans at Yorktown, Virginia. His surrender "turned the world upside down," effectively ending the American Revolutionary War. Here are the lyrics:

If buttercups buzzed after the bee,

If boats were on land, churches on sea,

If ponies rode men and if grass ate the cows,

And cats should be chased into holes by the mouse;

If mamas sold their babies

to Gypsies for half a crown,

If Summer were Spring

and the other way 'round;

Then all the world would be upside down!

☑

The Pledge of Allegiance and Flag Salute

I loved teaching my students about the pledge of allegiance, because it reminds us of all the blessings we enjoy as American citizens. It's easy to learn once the children understand its meaning:

I pledge ... I present my promise and devotion

allegiance ... my loyalty to our country

to the Flag ... our country's proud symbol

of the United States of America and to the republic for which it stands ... our republic, a group of 50 united states

one nation under God ... one country with God as our protector

indivisible ... our country cannot be divided

with liberty ... freedom

and justice ... treating all citizens equally according to our country's laws

for all ... Our laws guarantee and our country promises that all our citizens are the recipients of this liberty and justice.

History of the Pledge of Allegiance

The Pledge has undergone several changes since it was first introduced in 1892 by a children's magazine celebrating the four hundredth anniversary of the discovery of the Americas by Columbus. In 1923, the words "my flag" were placed by "the flag of the United States." A year later, the words "of America" were added. The pledge was approved by Congress in 1942. In 1954, in an effort to distinguish the United States from the officially atheist Soviet Union, with whom the country was engaged in a cold war, the words, "under God" were inserted into the Pledge.

Presently, pending lawsuits would, if won, remove the words, "under God." (Wikipedia.org)

Students help Stan Cody (in Uncle Sam's patriotic costume) raise the American flag.

Stan's Out-of-the-Box Stories

New is Not Always Better

About every four or five years, the state selection board for new schoolbooks lifts its head out of the dark recesses and informs the public they are doing their job. They do this by letting schools spend large sums of money on new school books. Reading book revampment is my pet peeve.

In the short span of four years, stories that were once wonderful are no longer of interest or value to the students. I understand that books do get worn and torn, but must we discard some of the best stories forever?

I spotted this malfunction in my first year of teaching. When it occurred, I compared the books that had been used for the previous four years with the new books. Yes, there were great stories in both, but one book was not better than the other. Some stories in the new books were just plain boring.

I trotted down to the school district book reserve where most of the books were archived for several years. Wowee! What I found there excited me. Would you believe that I found seven complete class sets of reading books? Each set had perfect jewels – stories that always drew and maintained high interest among students.

I asked if I could borrow them and was told, "They're yours. Take them. We never want to see them again." I grabbed them and ran.

Where am I going with this tale? I'm going to the FUN LAND OF GREAT READING STORIES. In our leisure time, do we as adults continue to read a story if it is boring? Of course not. Then why do we expect our students to read boring stories?

I was ready for bear and my ammunition consisted of many sets of fantastic stories that children loved. Even though some of these books had been written as long ago as the 1950s, children still found them exciting.

Things don't always work out as we hope they will. One day, we were reading a story about moving west in pilgrim days. I had only read the first three pages. It sounded great, so we began reading aloud. While the students took turns reading, I skipped ahead to get a quick look at the ending. Wow. Electric chills went down my spine. The story's conclusion included a conversation between two wagon train leaders about a wagon train of Mormons that had just crossed the Platte River. Their words were laden with prejudice, and I immediately asked the class to stop reading so I could explain what I'd discovered.

The story was inappropriate for us to read,

and the discovery led to an interesting class discussion of prejudice and fairness. I finished by asking my students if they would like to participate in ridding the world of a little prejudice. They look at me rather quizzically. I tore a page from my out-of-date book. As I shook my head and muttered, "Yes, yes, yes," I tore more pages from that particular story in the book. The students reacted with great surprise at first and then they caught on. One of the girls smiled and tore a page from her book. The others followed.

Oh, did the class have fun obliterating prejudice by destroying that story! Some students made confetti from their pages. Our room looked like Times Square in New York City on New Year's Eve.

Although we kept using the book for the great value of other solid, non-prejudicial stories within its pages, I refused to push my students to read material that I would not read. And thus, my reading classes enjoyed great success.

And I didn't mind at all pushing the vacuum cleaner to rid the room of all the paper confetti and save the custodian the trouble.☑

Colonies, States and British Laws

The Original Thirteen Colonies

If you learn the following silly sentence word for word and use only the words beginning with capital letters, you will have all of the original thirteen colonies represented in order, from South to North. So it's a great geography lesson, tooooooooo!

Georgia and Stan Cody* Never Considered Virginia to be a Medical Doctor in a Deli because Nothing Jived in Pa's Connection of Riding In a New York Mass of Homes.

*Replace my name with your own or Santa

Clause or any two words beginning with the letters S *and* C.

The previous statement is taught to help children learn the states as follows:

Georgia	= Georgia
Stan Cody	= South Carolina
Never Considered	= North Carolina
Virginia	= Virginia
Medical	= Maryland
Deli	= Delaware
Nothing Jived	= New Jersey
Pa's	= Pennsylvania
Connection	= Connecticut
Riding In	= Rhode Island
New York	= New York
Mass	= Massachusetts
New Homes	= New Hampshire

Early civil rights leader Susan B. Anthony was a frequent characterization by Stan.

Confederate States of America

Eleven states left the Union during the Civil War. The following sentence helps students remember the geography of the United States during this historic era. The recitation begins with seven southern and Gulf Coast states or South Carolina, Georgia, Florida, Alabama, Mississippi, Louisiana and Texas, then jumps up to Arkansas, east to Virginia, south to North Carolina, and finally circles around to Tennessee.

South Carolina and Georgia Found Alabama's Missing Lions, Tigers, Aardvarks and Vicious Non-conforming Teddy-bears.

South Carolina
Georgia
Florida
Alabama
Mississippi
Louisiana
Texas
Arkansas
Virginia
North Carolina
Tennessee

A little trivia for you: The Confederate flag displayed thirteen stars representing thirteen states, but only eleven states actually left the Union to join the Confederacy. Both Missouri and Kentucky failed to follow through on their intention to secede from the Union.

Voting in the Colonies

In the early days of our United States, only free white males who owned land and were 21 years of age or older were permitted to vote. (Haven't we come a long way?!) Here's a story and exercise that helped my students learn these five stringent requirements:

It was a beautiful, balmy Spring day, as Tommy sat at the kitchen table eating his mashed potatoes. The kitchen window was open and the curtains blew gently in the breeze as he dipped his fork one more time into the fluffy white mound on his plate. Tommy's meal was interrupted when he heard the singing of a bird outside the window. He looked

Stan, portraying General Robert E. Lee, with companion in Civil War attire.

up and saw the bird. As he watched, the bird flew away and a feather floated through the air, into the window and landed on his mashed potatoes. When his mother called, "How are you eating your mashed potatoes, Tommy?" Tommy replied, "With The Feather On Mashed Potatoes, Mom."

This story is a way of setting the scene for a mnemonic that teaches students the requirements for voting in the early days of our country:

With The Feather On Mashed-Potatoes.

W = White
T = Twenty-one
F = Free
O = Owned land
M = Male

Introducing the Acts

Several laws were passed by the British parliament to provide for the supply and well-being of the British government's troops in the United States. They included:

Quartering Act

The Quartering Act was passed by the British Parliament in 1765 to regulate the payment, quartering (residence), marching and supplies of soldiers in the colonies.

"Bring Cody's Firewood Very Soon" describes the soldiers' supplies furnished by each family:

B = Bed
C = Candles
F = Firewood
V = Vinegar
S = Supplies

Stamp Act

This act regulated the granting and applying of stamp duties (fees), and other duties, in the British colonies and plantations of America, and for amending parts of Parliamentary acts that related to the trade and revenues of the colonies and plantations, to recover penalties and forfeitures. The taxes were intended to help pay for the Seven Years War. They were applied to purchases of the following goods. Here's a mnemonic to help remember the Stamp Act: *News A Drunk Duck (stamped) Paper Cards.*

N	= News	= Newspapers
A	= A	= Almanacs
D	= Drunk	= Liquor
D	= Duck	= Documents
(stamped)		= Stamp Act
P	= Paper	= Documents and Cards

Townshend Act

Named after British treasurer Charles Townshend. The Townshend Act taxed colonists on: Lead, Paint, Tea, Glass and Paper. Here's the Townshend mnemonic, reading as if it were a sentence: *Lead Paint The Green Paper*

Colony Cards Trivia

The colonists' playing cards were circular in shape. They refused to play with the cards from England, because they displayed pictures of a King, Queen and Jack, representing royalty. The colonists made their own cards and used pictures of an Indian Chief, a squaw and a brave.

Stan's Out-of-the-Box Stories

A Salute to the Teacher

I'm really proud of this story written by Nancy Sullivan, the mother of one of my eighth grade students:

My daughter, Katie Sullivan, had Mr. Cody as her U.S. History teacher at La Paz Intermediate School for the 1995-96 school year. After a couple of months of attending high school the following year, she told me:

"Mom, I now know what the only problem of having Mr. Cody as a teacher was."

What was that?, I asked Katie.

"Well, once you have had Mr. Cody, you will never have anyone as good ever again," *she replied.*

I love it when the parents and the students are happy. This is a nice compliment and I am sure it comes from the heart. It's the experience Katie had in my classroom that inspired her to say such nice things to her mother.

I demanded a lot from my students and they gave it to me. Yes, it was a lot of work. It took considerable thought, planning and preparation. But I LOVED it! And because I loved it, my students connected with me and with each other. My students also loved learning.

And that is the secret to engaging the minds of your students. ☑

More Fun for Teachers and Students

From Presidents to Baseball & The Science Song

Here's something that I guarantee will be fun for your class. On lists that your students MUST learn, help them make up their own acronymal sentences. This is fairly easy to do and fun, especially if you follow these basic guidelines:

- Creating the mnemonic will be easier if the words are not required to follow a precise order.

- Include vowels so the sentence or mnemonic flows easily and seems logical.

- Make sure all of the important words are capitalized and words that are not part of the acronym, but are necessary as connectors, are in lower case.

- Students should not be required to share their words or sentences. Those who wish to share theirs may, but sharing is not a requirement. They create them to help themselves learn.

- Just for practice, write a sentence using these words: Steal, Will, Footballs, Girls, Apricots, Envelopes

My version might have looked like this:

Every Girl Will Find Sweet Apricots; or

Even Athletic Girls Will Steal Footballs

Now write a sentence with a related acronym to help you remember an event or sequence of events.

Batting the Baseball Correctly

This mnemonic, as seen on the popular television series, "Monk", is easy to remember as you're standing in the batter's box because it conjures up a picture:

H = Hands together
E = Elbow up
L = Level swing
P = Patience

The Great Lakes

Just spell HOMES:

H = Huron
O = Ontario

M = Michigan
E = Erie
S = Superior

Remembering our Presidents

Learning the names of more than 40 presidents in the order they served our country can be a daunting task. But not to worry! Break the list into four groups and devise a memorable sentence for each group. Try these – or create your own:

With A Jolly Mad Mongoose Apple Jumping Jackson's Volkswagen, Harrison Tied Pretty Tammy Fay, Pleasing Buchanan's Landlord.

Washington
Adams
Jefferson
Madison
Monroe
Adams
Jackson
Van Buren
Harrison
Tyler
Polk
Taylor
Fillmore
Pierce
Buchanan
Lincoln

Stan Cody dressed as George Washington, first president and considered the "father" of our country.

John Green Held Garfield And Charley Hog's Camel.

Johnson
Grant
Hayes
Garfield
Arthur
Cleveland
Harrison
Cleveland (second term)

Stan's Daniel Boone was always a hit with students.

McKinley Really Took Wilson's Hard Candy.

McKinley
Roosevelt
Taft
Wilson
Harding
Coolidge

Remember that President Taft came after President Theodore Roosevelt, not before, with: *Take Advice From Teddy (TAFT)* and you will be President.

The next set of presidents can be remembered with this silly saying:

Hoover Really Trusted Ike, Kennedy, Johnson (and) Nixon.

Hoover
Roosevelt, F.
Truman
Eisenhower

Kennedy
Johnson, L.
Nixon

Ford Cars Really Bank, Clinton Buick

Ford
Carter
Reagan
Bush, GH.
Clinton
Bush, GW.

When our next president takes office, just add that person's name to the end of the mnemonic

Presidential Powers

Who is the person who takes over the job of running the United States government when the president is too ill to do presidential duties, is dead or absent? If it is not possible for that person to take over, who is next in line to assume these duties? And next in line after that person? Let these mnemonics guide you. Use the first letter of each of these words to trigger the titles of next in line:

Very Politely, Speaker of the House P.S. Sillydog Threw Dear Alice's Horse Into Alligator Chomping Land.

Vice President (very politely) = first in line
Speaker of the House (speaker of the house) = second
President of the Senate (PS) = third
Secretary of State (Silly dog) = fourth

Secretary of the Treasury (Threw) = fifth
Secretary of Defense (Dear) = sixth
Attorney General (Alice's) = seventh
Secretary of Homeland Security (Horse) = eighth
Secretary of the Interior
(In) = ninth
Secretary of Agriculture
(Alligator) = tenth
Secretary of Commerce
(Chomping) = eleventh
Secretary of Labor (Land)
= twelfth

Note: The Secretary of Homeland Security was added to the mnemonic in 2005.

This batter needs help. Can you spot what's wrong with his batting position and explain why he's called a "cow-handed" batter? For the answer, turn to the end of the chapter.

Quick and Easily Remembered Facts

Who fought who in World War II?

JIG vs World = Japan, Italy, Germany vs World

The number and names of presidents who were killed while in office?

Assassination is when Men Kill Like Garfield. (presidents McKinley, Kennedy, Lincoln, Garfield)

Instructions given to Paul Revere:

One if by land, two if by sea: How do you remember which comes first? You learn to walk first (land), swim later (sea).

What did Frederick Douglass, a leader in the slavery abolition movement, name his newspaper?

The *North Star*, as it was the North Star that escaping slaves followed.

Which does the umpire of a baseball game call out first: Balls or strikes?

"B" (balls) comes before "S" (strikes) in the English alphabet.

The Star Spangled Parody (Song)

Although the words for the "Star Spangled Banner" were written in 1814 by Francis Scott Key, the tune came from an old English song called the "Anacrenotic Song." It was the theme song of the Anacrenotic Club, a men's club for affluent gentlemen who toasted and celebrated life, wine and making love.

Sharing this background will help students remember a colorful bit of history surrounding our country's national anthem. Although it is not necessary to teach students the words to the original tune, I'll share them here just to satisfy your curiosity:

To Anacrenon in Heaven, where he sat in full glee,

a few sons of harmony sent a petition

that he their inspirer and patron would be;

When this answer arrived from the jolly old Grecian:

"Voice, fiddle and flute, no longer be mute;
I'll lend you my name and inspire you to boot.
And besides, I'll instruct you, like me, to entwine
the myrtle of Venus with Bacchus's wine.

Principal or Principle?

Since the principal of your school should really be your pal, spell his title princi**pal.** (The word "principal"can also describe the first, highest or foremost in importance, rank, worth or degree; or the chief monetary amount in a financial transaction.)

If it's a lesson, a philosophy, a belief, a rule or such, spell it princi**ple.**

The Six Wives of Henry the Eighth

This little rhyming ditty that has floated around our schools for many years is still effective for learning the "endings" of the wives of Henry VIII:

Divorced, killed, died; divorced, killed, survived

Here's who did what:

Wife #1	Catherine of Aragon	Divorced
Wife #2	Ann Boleyn	Killed
Wife #3	Jane Seymour	Died
Wife #4	Ann of Cleves	Divorced
Wife #5	Catherine Howard	Killed
Wife #6	Catherine Parr	Survived

Note: Remove Wife #3 (the wife who died), and all will be in alphabetical order.

Those teaching in faith-based schools may appreciate the following memorics and find them helpful:

The Ten Commandments

The Ten Commandments can be an excellent code of morality and ethics for humankind. Full of visual imagery, it's easy to write mnemonics and statements to aid in remembering them:

Never In Victor's Sweet Home (did) Kelly Admit Stealing From Charles.

N = <u>No</u> other Gods before me

I = No graven <u>Images</u>, none

V = Do not take the name of the Lord in <u>Vain</u>

S = Remember the <u>Sabbath</u> Day, to keep it holy

H = <u>Honor</u> your father and mother

K = Do not <u>Kill</u>

A = Do not commit <u>Adultery</u>

S = Do not <u>Steal</u>

F = Do not bear <u>False</u> witness against your neighbor

C = Do not <u>Covet</u> your neighbor's possessions

The Cain and Abel Lesson

Do you want an easy way to remember who was the firstborn son, Cain or Abel? Or which son was the first one to be killed and by whom? Do your students find it hard to remember which son was the shepherd and which one the farmer?

This is really easy, especially if you know a little about farming in the midwestern United States.

A is the first letter of our alphabet. That makes it simple to remember that Abel was the firstborn son of Adam and Eve.

Cain killed Abel. That's easy to learn if you picture Cain killing Abel with his cane.

Cane (a little different spelling than Cain's name) describes a crop grown on farms especially for fodder/feed for cattle in the heartland of our country. Pair the two – Cain with the crop cane – and you've got the son who was the farmer. That leaves Abel as the shepherd.

The Science Song

Here's a song I wrote to help children learn about the cycle of life. Sing it to the tune of, "We Three Kings of Orient Are:"

The world is made of litter and duff,
Humus and top soil and all that good stuff,
Producer, consumer and decomposer
Is known as the cycle of life.
Oooooh Oooooh,

The world was put here for us to use,
Not to tear up or to abuse;
If we abuse it, we will lose it,
Don't be an old dumb-dumb!

Lyrics by Stanley W. Cody

Play on Words

Have some fun with word sounds and spellings!

When you pronounce the letters S O C K S aloud, reciting each letter by itself, it sounds like "esso si que es," which means "That's the way it is," in Spanish.

Earthworm Hearts

The earthworm has five hearts and they are located in the seventh, eighth, ninth, tenth and eleventh segments. Your students might remember this with the aid of this tale: *I found my heart in the Seven Eleven store. You'll find it in segments (aisles) seven through eleven.*

Rainbow Colors

Here's the mnemonic for the colors of the rainbow: *Richard Of York Gave Battle In Vain.*

R = Red
O = Orange
Y = Yellow
G = Green
B = Blue
I = Indigo
V = Violate

ROY G. BIV is another widely used acronym for the colors of the rainbow: red, orange, yellow, green, blue, indigo and violet. A fellow named Greg Crowther has written a song that tells the tale of a man named Roy G. Biv, using all the colors of the rainbow, who, over the course of his rather bizarre life, experiences the full spectrum of what the world has to offer. See the ballad and meet Greg Crowther at http://faculty.washington.edu/crowther/Misc/Songs/roygbiv.shtml.

Poisonous and Non-poisonous Snakes

Here's how to tell if a snake is a poisonous coral snake or not:

- Yellow or white on red, and you're dead.
- White or yellow surrounding red, stay away.
- Any snake in North America that has catlike eyes is poisonous.

Having Some Fun With Horsengoggling

There's a popular method of "counting" to determine who will end up the winner, that goes: "Eeenie, meany, miney, moe; catch a tiger by the toe; if he hollers, make him pay fifteen dollars every day." Using the "Eenie, meany, miney, moe" approach, the intelligent student can determine precisely where he should stand in order to win a prize. If he's in the number 22 spot, he wins.

With the game of Horsengoggle, it is impossible for the student to predict where he should stand in order to win. The game is played like this:

Have all the students line up. Tell them who you are going to start counting from. Then, at the signal, "Ein, Stein, Swine, Horsengoggle," ask the students to raise their hands and extend one, two, three, four or five fingers.

Count the extended fingers of the entire group and note the total of all the fingers.

After announcing the total, begin counting student by student, until the total number is reached. (If you count each student and have not reached the total number, continue counting from the beginning of the line again.)

The lucky, prize-winning student is the one with whom the total number is reached.

If you're awarding prizes, give the next two or three prizes to the students with the next numbers; or play the game again. (Most students like to play the game again, but the decision about consecutive games must be made before the original game is played.)

This works much better than the tired old "eeny meeny miney moe."

Fun with Cards

Here's another way to choose the student to answer the next questions.

Using a standard deck of cards, write each student's name on two cards. Shuffle and cut the deck. Ask a question. Pull a card to see whose name comes up. Once that student has answered the question, insert his or her card back into the deck. Shuffle and cut the deck again and draw for the next student's name.

It's possible to keep calling the same student's name, and that's part of the fun of the game.

> ***Answer to the baseball batter question*** *(see cartoon earlier in chapter): Any batter is called a "cow-handed" batter if he has the "wrong" hand on top when batting. For a proper swing, the "power" hand (the dominant hand) should always be on the top. Notice our cartoon shows a left-handed batter facing the pitcher, with his hands in the incorrect position.*

Stan's Out-of-the-Box Stories

Stan's Successful Students

Oh, I have had some interesting students over my 33-year teaching career. How about two who ultimately earned Super Bowl rings? Or those who became the head secretary to three United States ambassadors, a senator, a mayor, scientists and business owners. Quentin Tarantino got his film start in my sixth grade science (more later in the book). Yes, he was cool even then. Out of the box? I think so.

Stan's Not So Successful Students

I can't brag to you about the heights of success to which some of my students have risen unless I also mention that one of my former students tried to hire a "hit man" to kill her husband. I have no idea when she'll be released from prison, if ever. But, when she

English Learning Shortcuts

Nouns, Vowels & Other English Characters

Some kids take to English like a duck to water. It comes naturally to them. They discover that proper English, including grammar, sentence structure and punctuation, is almost intuitive. Other kids find English highly challenging, unnatural and difficult to grasp.

Each year in my teaching career brought new students to my English class. Each new group brought a nonverbal level of communication that I could truly feel at the gut level.

I was never good in English. I didn't understand it until my college days and, because I didn't understand it, I just kind of gave up on the whole subject. We diagrammed sentences and then diagrammed more sentences. To this day, I feel that teaching this skill to fourth, fifth and sixth graders is a waste of time and a true obstacle to learning. Many times, when students don't grasp the concept, the teacher persists, believing the student will eventually catch on. But the student may learn only enough to pass the test and never really understand the lesson.

No wonder my favorite "subject" was recess! I understood the rules to that game, and isn't that what diagramming sentences is about? Understanding the rules is key.

Girls in my class were really good at diagramming. Maybe that's because their right brain thinking kicked in with a good overall picture of sentence structuring. Maybe it was because of their intuitive abilities or their left brain's logic and analytics helped them hone these tasks skillfully. Girls seemed to have an affinity for words and relationships of words with each other.

The English language is both beautiful and confusing. I'm just grateful that I was able to communicate the lessons using tools and mental tricks that helped my students overcome inherent challenges.

Each year on my first real teaching day of class (not the day or arrival when seat were assigned and books and preliminaries were addressed), I surprised my students by saying, "English is the second hardest language to learn if it is your second language; but it can be a lot of fun." (According to linguists and etymologists concerned with the history of words, English is second only to the Vietnamese language, when trying to learn it as a second language.)

Why is English difficult to learn? It's the enormous collection of words derived from many other languages. Every day, English-speaking people use words (often within the same sentences) with historical roots in several languages. For example, there are words with European origins (house, apple, mayonnaise), Latin (asthma, hospital, humor), Arabic (hazard, saffron, zero), Chinese (lemon) and the Romance languages (romance, avocado, chocolate). Many of our words evolved through several different languages to find their place in English.

My students were intrigued with the idea that it's possible for a simple sentence to have two completely different meanings. It's also possible for a sentence to have two totally different meanings when all its letters are in the exact order but placed with the wrong word.

Here's an example of a simple sentence with two different meanings: *Paige is out walking her dog Skip.*

If I ask you to draw a picture representing that statement, you will probably draw a girl holding onto a leash attached to Skip's collar, with Skip walking ahead of her.

But that's not at all what I meant by that sentence. If Paige is out walking the dog, Paige is walking in front of the dog. If the dog is being walked, it is behind her, following her.

Of course, on a humorous note, I could have said that the dog was out walking his owner, in which case Skip would be walking ahead of Paige. Or I could have said that Paige is "out-walking" her dog, which gives their walk a competitive angle and makes it sound like Paige is able to walk faster than her dog.

Here's another example: *Megan is now here.*

Putting a space in the wrong place but in its intended order could cause the sentence to mean the opposite, like this: *Megan is no where.*

Then we have a couple of examples where you can tell a lie by telling the truth. A lie is a statement that attempts to communicate the opposite of the truth. Since I'm a storyteller at heart, I've created my examples in stories

Mr. Cody robs a store

Mr. Cody, a most loved teacher, made a special stop at a little convenience store on his way home from teaching evening classes at school. He decided to rob the store, hoping he wouldn't be recognized by several of his students who were busy chatting with each other outside the building.

The hold-up went fine but as Mr. Cody ran from the store afterward, he tripped and fell and dropped all the cash. Silver coins and greenbacks of all denominations went flying across the parking lot.

Mr. Cody's students saw him fall and ran to his aid. As they picked up the money and tried to help him, one of them naively mentioned, "I didn't know the ATMs would give out this much cash at one time!"

Hurriedly getting into his car, Mr. Cody replied jokingly, "Naaaw, they don't. I just robbed the store."

All the students laughed and said in unison, "Sure, Mr. Cody, sure."

Benjamin Franklin, a public servant who wore many hats, including author, publisher, abolitionist, printer, philanthropist and more.

Did the students believe Mr. Cody? He told the truth; but he also told a lie. He got them to believe something that was true really wasn't true.

In the next story, you'll be the person telling the lie. But first, here are some things you need to know.

Into the Civil War at age eighteen

During the Civil War, both the North and the South wanted and needed soldiers desperately. Volunteers were required to be at least eighteen years of age to sign up to serve in the military forces. Back then, a man's word was his soul. If he gave his word that something was true, you could rely upon it being true.

If a young man had not yet become eighteen but wanted to enlist to help his side win the war, he used a little trick in order to appear to tell the truth about his age. Before joining volunteers lined up to join the troops, he took off his shoes. Off to the side, where he couldn't be seen, he took out a pencil and wrote the number 18 on the sole of each of his shoes.

Later, as he stood in line and his turn came up, the enlisting officer inquired, "Are you over eighteen?" The young man replied confidently, "Yes," knowing that he was over the "18" written under his feet. And then he assured the officer, "I guarantee you that I am over 18."

Did he tell the truth? Yes, he did.

Did he deceive and get the man to believe something that was not true? Yes, he did. Although he was over "18," he told a lie.

While I'm at it, let me just toss one more example in to show how people sometimes tell a story that appears on the surface to be telling the truth when, in fact, it steers the listener away from the truth.

Who stole from the cookie jar?

Jimmy wanted a cookie badly, but he and his brother Bobby had been told by their mother that they were not to touch the cookie jar before dinner. Jimmy could taste the chocolate chips, could feel them melting in his mouth, the sweet, chocolatey flavor caressing his tongue. But, even though cookies had been mysteriously disappearing from the cookie jar for some time, the cookie jar was off limits!

No one would know if he took one cookie, Jimmy reasoned as he snuck quietly across the kitchen to the big red strawberry-shaped jar. He reached in, grabbed a cookie and quickly devoured it.

Dinnertime arrived and the family began its evening social time, sharing the events of the day with each other. Jimmy was silent until it became obvious he wasn't talking. Then he piped up with, "Aren't you glad that Bobby didn't take any cookies from the cookie jar again today?"

Immediately, Mom saw Bobby as the cookie thief. Jimmy's little trick worked and he got away with it, creating a lie by deflecting the facts.

Stories and mnemonics engage the mind

America's early day trappers blazed the trails of civilization.

Students connect with stories and understand story examples. That's what teaching is all about: Presenting material in a way that connects the student and the material, generates interest and results in participatory learning. When you come up with one of these little gems (as silly as mine, sillier or serious), write them down so you can use them again and again. Please share your stories and examples with me, and I'll share them with the world of education through my website and give you the credit.

Think these stories are too ridiculous? I've been cautioned numerous times that the students would not participate in certain exercises. I just love it when people challenge me like that! There have been a few times when my ideas have failed, but not very often.

Perhaps now I have aroused your interest as I did that of my students. Good! You're in a great position to share your excitement with your students and help them understand why it's so important to study English, to be attentive and get it right.

You've probably experienced talking with someone who did not appear to be really listening. Sometimes, I stop talking and say, "Wait! I don't think we are communicating here," and then I try again.

The avalanche of information coming at us *every* day has made it difficult for us to focus, to listen and to hear. It's a problem we are all dealing with. Songs and stories help us zoom past the blurr of information to learn good language skills.

Stan Cody portrays the Blacksmith of Brandywine, the essential blacksmith and farrier who shoed the horses and helped keep America moving.

Parts of speech

Try this mnemonic: *The people's favorite king was PAN CAP IV.*

P = pronoun
A = adverb
N = noun
C = conjunction
A = adjective
P = preposition

I = interjection
V = verb

Nouns and pronouns

When sung to the tune of "Auld Lang Syne," the stories and melodies that follow can be an enjoyable and effective way for students to learn about nouns and pronouns.

The Dollar Bill Exercise

Before I begin the dollar bill exercise, I ask the class to define a noun and a pronoun. I ask them to raise their hands if they know the answers. Then I ask, "How many will accept an A for the class if you are absolutely correct and a D if your answer is incorrect?" Boy, the hands drop like hailstones.

Finally, some brave soul raises his or her hand and states their definition of a pronoun. It may be correct or close to correct, but I usually say, No, and I proceed to explain that a pronoun is a noun that "works" for living.

Then I tell a little story and use a visual aid. I tack or tape a dollar bill to the chalkboard and tell the students that one of them will win it. Aha! Now they're all ears, all eyes. I've connected! Even the rowdiest members of my class are tuned in. (Successful teaching needs this sort of attention, possible only through connection. And when you get the poor and rowdy students' attention, others follow their lead.)

Then, I define noun and pronoun by writing on the board:

A noun's a person, place or thing;
A person, place or thing.
A noun's a person, place or thing,
A person, place or thing.

Then I tell this story to illustrate the noun-pronoun concept:

Wagon Trail Nouns and Pronouns

The year was 1856. Arnus, Letty, their five-year-old son Jeb and four-week-old daughter Kennedy were on their way to a new and better life in the Oregon Territory.

The family had sold nearly everything they owned back East. In preparation for their journey to the West Coast, they had purchased a Conestoga wagon, livestock and months' worth of supplies, tools and food. Travel was rough, as they followed the train of wagons through rough terrain, forded rivers and traversed mountain passes and deserts. Finally, after several months, they found themselves on the north side of the Platte River in Nebraska, a few days away from their destination.

As the wagon train rolled slowly over a little rise in the prairie, the wagon master noticed a large herd of buffalo moving south on a course with the trail. In the face of danger and inevitable collision with the herd, the wagon master yelled to his wagon team leaders to "Move 'em out!"

This, of course, meant "Put the horses in high gear! Pull them into a run!"

Like most wagon trails, this one had many ruts and bumps that made the wagons bounce wildly.

Pots and pans and other supplies were thrown about and those riding had to hold on for dear life. Little Jeb got very excited with all the commotion. Arnus and Letty, trying very hard to keep the wagon under control as it raced with the others to beat the buffalo, didn't pay much attention to Jeb until he began to holler loudly.

Finally, when the wagons were out of danger and had slowed, they tried to understand what Jeb was saying. But the little guy was so excited, he could barely speak. Remembering how Jeb loved to sing and how, on many occasions, Jeb had calmed himself by singing, Arnus asked Jeb to sing what he was trying to say. The words rippled forth from Jeb's mouth to the tune of "Auld Lang Syne."

A baby is a wondrous thing
to have in all our lives
But, Daddy, Kennedy fell out the back
and she's three miles behind.

When I sang that last line to the class, they reacted spontaneously with laughter. I wrote the words on the board and then I instructed them to read the words as I sang them. Finally, I taped another dollar bill to the board and renewed their attention.

"We're all going to sing the first verse together," I said, pointing to the board. We sang the song three times and then we changed the words to:

When the Nouns get sick
The Pros come in
Such as I, Me, You, He, Him
She, Her, It, We, Us, You and They
and sometimes also Them.

The students then wrote the song in their notes, to help them firmly cement it in their heads.

I've used stories and songs many times, for grades five through twelve, and it has always worked well. It also works wonders with a dollar bill.

After singing, I would divide the class into three groups. Then, together as a whole group, we sang the second verse to the song several times; and then each group sang the verse separately.

I then place a ten dollar bill way high on the board, off to the right or left, without explaining why.

After the entire class had sung the song about three more times, each group sang it individually as loudly as they could, shouting, to see who would represent each group in the run off competition. (The loudest singer in each group became the representative.)

When three finalists emerged, I asked each to sing the song as loudly as possible. The class voted to determine who sang the loudest with no mistakes.

The two dollar bills were awarded to the winner. Yes, you guessed it: "What about the ten dollar bill?," they asked. Then with a slight smile, I would tell them that ten dollar bill was just weighing a little heavily in my pocket and I put it up there so I could rest awhile.

Believe me, it took an entire class session, but this taught each and every student the definition of a noun and a pronoun, and the meanings were theirs for life. It cost me five classes of two dollars each, but it was worth the effort and the added connection with my students.

Prepositions

A preposition is a word that an airplane can do to a cloud:

The airplane can go in, around, through, by, over, under, etc., a cloud.

Vowels

Use a simple sentence that places the vowels in alphabetical order:

Students A, E, I, O and U went dancing and sometimes they even invited W and Y to go with them.

Or try this:

Amy Often Ignored Ellen While Unconsciously Yawning.

Adjectives

Sing this ditty to the chorus of "Waltzing Matilda:"

Adjective, oh adjective, give me some adjectives

to tell me what the nouns in our crazy song are like

And use colors, texture, numbers and words that end in BLE,

You'll know that adjectives describe all the nouns.

Sing this to the verse portion of "Waltzing Matilda" (or write your own) (the adjectives are underlined):

Once a cute brown bunny rabbit ran out of his cozy hole,

He ran 'till he found the cabbage patch, you see,

It was big and it was green and it was full of yummy food for him;

Thank you, mister farmer, for giving me this food.

Conjunctions

A conjunction can be remembered by using the word *fanboys* (a term that originated in comic book circles and describes a young man who is totally devoted to a subject). The following list does not include all conjunctions but gives the students a good start.

Fanboys

F = for
A = and
N = nor
B = but
O = or
Y = yet
S = so

A conjunction is also referred to as a "joiner," because it "joins" ideas and statements together, as in:

The girls beat the boys and then the boys beat the girls.

Common Determiners

This is a challenge for the students, to see who can recite the list of common determiners the fastest, without making an error. It's a little like the 1980s McDonald's commercial that went something like this: "Two all beef patties, special sauce, lettuce, cheese, pickles, onions on a sesame seed bun." Used with a stop watch, it goes like this:

Common determiners are A, AND, THE. Other words often used as determiners are THIS, THAT, THESE, THOSE SOME, FEW, MOST, MANY, ALL BOTH, EACH, EVERY, ANY, HIS, HER, ITS, OUR MY and numbers 1, 2, 3, 4 dot, dot, dot all on a sesame seed bun.

Most students were able with a little practice to say these without mistakes in around twelve seconds. Students love a challenge. In that they are learning a sentence for speed, they don't realize they are also learning the determiners.

Note: Examples and lists in this section are for illustration purposes. I expect you have much more material than what is presented here, that you can adapt in song and sentence, mnemonically, and so forth.

Stan loved to portray the Chinese coolie and would usually set up a laundry, such as those operated by Chinese immigrants during the Gold Rush era.

Stan's Out-of-the-Box Stories

The Best Day of School and the Worst Day of School

The two worst days of my school year, as a teacher, were always the first day and the last day. The first, be-cause I saw children crying and heard parents complaining that they couldn't get their child into my class; and the last  day of school because I was losing my family and I might not see them again ever (I do miss them).☑

This and That from Stan's Students, Family and Friends
Acronyms & Other Fun Memorics

I am always tickled and pleased when my students, children, grandchildren and others jump into the mnemonics and memory game with me. It's fun and the more, the merrier! I hope you enjoy these excellent and creative contributions as much as I have:

Spelling

When two vowels go a-walking, the first one does the talking.

The silent e makes the vowel say its name.

You can't spell "believe" without a "lie" in it.

Spell "arithmetic" with this mnemonic:

A Raccoon Is The Hottest Mammal Eating The Ice Cream.

Angles

An Acute Angle (<) is a cute little angle, less than 90 degrees. (Thank you, Scott Cody!)

Prefixes to Metric Measurements:

Kevin Howard Didn't Think That Drinking Cured Measels

K = Kevin
H = Howard
D = Didn't
T = Think (that)
D = Drinking
C = Cured
M = Measels

Roman Numerals

Lonely Children Drink Mustard.
L C D M

Spell the Word "Geometry"

Give Ellen Other Metric Examples 2 TRY

Spell the Word "Arithmetic"

A Racoon Is The Hottest Mammal Eating The Infantry's Corn

History

1821 was the date of the first free public school in America. To remember the year, say the following: I Eight a Number Two Pencil in "School." If you draw a pencil, instead of writing it out, it will look like 1821. (Thank you, Christy Cody.)

I 8 a #2   in school.

The Spelling of Mississippi

With "crooked letter" representing two S's and "humpback" representing the letter "P", say:

m i, crooked letter, i, crooked letter, i, humpback, humpback, i

Or spell the word and emphasize these under-lined characters:

m-i-s-s, i-s-s, i-p-p, i

The Seven Continents

Europe, Antarctica, Africa, Asia, Australia, North America, South America

An Adult Asian Never Eats Sour Aspirins

First Successful (Wright Brothers) Flight

The Wright brothers had glee in 1903.

Two Large Birds

The Ostrich, the largest bird in the world, has two toes on each foot. The Emu, which looks like an ostrich, has three toes.

To remember the most obvious difference between the two, just turn the "E" in Emu into a "3" and make it "3mu". (Thanks, Jennifer and Skipper.)

The Four Oceans

Indian Ocean, Atlantic Ocean, Arctic Ocean, Pacific Ocean

Indians Ate Pacific Artichokes

Stan's Out-of-the-Box Stories

Guillermo Teaches New Math

Because we really don't know everything, we might actually gain some knowledge from the students we teach. They offer wonderful insight.

In my first year of teaching, that wonderful "New Math" arrived. We'd been in school for about three months, when we came to  a particular math lesson. I understood it and explained it to the students.

When I'd finished, I asked if anyone had any questions. The students were absolutely silent. I said, "O.K., get busy."

Then Emily raised her hand and said, "I don't know how to do it."

I looked up and asked if there was anyone who could explain it to Emily.

No one raised a hand.

So, I went over the lesson again and still, no one knew what was going on. I went over it again. Still, the faces were blank.

Then I simply asked if anyone knew how to do the assignment. Guillermo raised his hand, so I asked Guillermo if he would teach the class. He nodded affirmatively, so I handed him the chalk. In two minutes, using the same general language I had used, Guillermo explained the lesson in a way that his classmates understood.

Sometimes kids just communicate differently and on the same level as their classmates. ☑

Advanced Challenges
for Students

Sometimes kids surprise us by achieving results their parents or teachers were unwilling to work toward or felt were "impossible" for the students to achieve.

One year, I requested funds from our school's parent-teacher organization to purchase 8 millimeter film (the old kind of film that had to be loaded and then turned over for recording on the reverse side) so my sixth grade students could create their own movies. The PTA did not approve the funds. They considered the purchase wasteful, so I purchased the film myself. We decided to show the PTA that the investment was for a good thing.

The students, working in groups of three, made excellent little movies, some of which included musical backgrounds. The members of the PTA, who had approved many other projects without blinking an eye, were quite impressed when they saw what the class accomplished. (As I mentioned earlier in this book, successful film director Quentin Tarantino* was in this class and got his start with this movie project.) In the end, the PTA paid for the film.

Dan Robbins, band teacher at La Paz Intermediate School, extends these sorts of "adult" level challenges to his students regularly. He'll say to his band members, "I think this music may be too hard for you. Maybe you should wait until you get into high school." Guess what? His students always learned the material.

Recently, at a Music Challenge competition at Southern California's Magic Mountain amusement park, Dan completed the high school level paperwork by mistake (instead of the junior high forms). When the awards were handed out, his kids had won all five events – in the high school division. What a teacher! Dan Robbins accomplishes incredible feats with his students because he challenges them.

Challenge your students. You'll be pleasantly and incredibly surprised.

Tarantino made his first film, a sequel to "The Poseidon Adventure," on regular 8mm film in this class project.

Stan's Out-of-the-Box Stories

Be Careful What You Promise
(The Dollar Bill Promise)

As an added incentive for a sixth grade math test, I announced that I would put three dollars on the board and that some lucky student would win them. (I did not say the student with a perfect score would win them.)

The test required the adding of simple proper fractions with common denominators: 1/6 + 1/6 and 3/6 + 1/6. We'd covered

this lesson for two days and all students had been present. They were all prepared for the ten math problems. They all should have gotten a perfect score.

Under the money, I put two 3x5" index cards, but no one could see what was written on them. I wrote on the board that the winner would get the money but would have to read the two cards in front of the class.

Good. No problem, right?

Wrong!

I gave the test and, out of 34 pupils, 33 got a perfect score of ten.

The one who did not get a perfect score was Tommy, who got only one answer correct. Tommy just didn't seem to care about anything in life.

With 33 perfect scores, who would get the money? I asked a student to read the instruction card. It said the winner would be the person who missed the most problems. So, Tommy came to the board and proudly announced that he had missed nine of the math problems. Before I could stop him, he read the other note to the class.

Hold on now. This is what Tommy read: "This (money) is for the person who missed any of the problems, as he will need it when he gets out of school, because he doesn't know math."

Completely unaffected by the message on the card, Tommy stuffed the money into his pocket, smiled, said, "Thank You," and sat down.

This is not the outcome I'd hoped for, of course, but you know, I did get 33 students to really try hard and they did succeed.

But I don't like to put a student down. There's never a good reason for it. Fortunately, Tommy wasn't bothered by the experience. I called his mother and explained the situation and she assured me all was fine.

I saw Tommy later that day and he was holding a gallon of ice cream. (I wonder where he got the money?) ☑

Lesson Plans
Make Your Own Butter, Build a Wickiup, Play Boxingball

Activities and lesson plans really must be your own, because your personality and your techniques are the ones that will make your activities work for you. I'll share a few of mine with you. They'll inspire you and you can use them as starting points.

Every child wants to be involved. Select different students for different activities or parts of an activity. Entice students with low or borderline academic standings to participate. They may not be able to excel in certain academic subjects but in a group activity, it's their time to be in the limelight and shine.

Caution/Warning

Some of the exercises published in this chapter and elsewhere in the book involve the use of food and some pretty delectable food dishes. But there are laws governing the preparation and serving of food. To comply, do not allow your students to taste any of the foods you prepare. Likewise, for safety sake, do not allow the students to use sharp utensils and cutting tools. (Please be sure to read my *Warnings and Cautions* chapter.)

Stan's Out-of-the-Box Stories

In the Limelight

The term, "in the limelight," originated in the mid-1800s on the English stage. Scottish surveyor and politician Thomas Drummond had invented limelight in 1825, by burning calcium oxide (lime) in a hot hydrogen-oxygen flame that distributed a brilliant white light for lighthouses and surveying crews. Safer than  gaslight, theaters soon began to replace unsafe gaslights with limelights to light up the activities taking place on the stage. Limelights were replaced eventually with electric lights.

☑

The Speed of Light

Several times while teaching Science to my fourth, fifth and sixth graders, I got them to remember the speed of light with a simple, easy-to-do trick.

I took them to the playground and we formed two lines. Now the speed of light is 186,284 miles per second (although it's typically quoted as 186,000). Every time I called, "speed," the students yelled 186,284. Then I'd say, "What's that?" They answered, "That's the speed." And I'd ask, "Of what?," and they would reply, "The speed of light." At that point, in unison, they would say, loudly, "186,284 miles per second the speed of light!"

The students could not predict when I'd say the word, "speed." We must have been on the playground for about ten minutes, as we formed two lines and serpentined through the swings, slides and play equipment. They never missed a beat and I'll bet that short ten-minute playground lesson is still with them.

What was so fascinating that day, as it was on many days, is that the students all participated in an activity they enjoyed, an activity that helped them learn. In the days to come, they reported back to me what other kids said when they learned of the playground fun. I would just look at them and wink. We all knew they had fun while they learned.

Build a Wickiup (Ancient Indian House)

In my sixth grade class, we made an ancient house in the same way the early Indians made theirs.

A creek flowed just below our playground area, offering a perfect spot to gather material for this exercise. With permission from the school principal and their parents, six students and I went to the creek during lunch break and cut long, slender and very flexible willow twigs for the project.

It took the class about a week to finish the project. We made a circle on the ground and stuck the poles deep into the ground along the circle line. The long saplings were then shaped to create a frame, like a geodesic dome, meeting and fastened together at the top.

We tied the real thin willow saplings around the outside. Once the framework was complete, we attached a water repellent cloth/tarp and moved the wikiup into the classroom. (You can get more detailed instructions at *http://www.texasindians.com/wickiup.htm.*)

The students worked hard to get all their classwork done quickly after that, because the reward was the opportunity to sit inside the wickiup, after we had moved it into the classroom.

Build a Pyramid

Make a pyramid by stacking shoe boxes. Add some "reality" with rubber spiders and snakes.

Build a Cabin

My students loved building an early American log cabin with Lincoln Logs[R]. We had a huge supply of Lincoln Logs in a big box on one side of the room. We designated a spot across the room as our cabin-building locations. Upon his turn, each child was instructed to go to the log box, pick up one log, carry it to his group's cabin-building spot and position it where it best fits in the building. This exercise taught the students about the homes in which our forefathers and pioneers lived. It also taught them about the methods of construction used at that time, with interlocking pieces. Best of all, it taught them how to work together toward a group goal.

Tar and Feather for Effect

Let's say you are teaching about the old punishment technique of smearing a body with tar, then sprinkling it with feathers (which the victim was unable to shed for days). This practice was used to punish delinquents and was often administered against British tax collectors who tried to enforce the Townshend Acts. Tar and feathering presents a fascinating wordpicture, so why not demonstrate it with some visuals?

Get an inexpensive toy doll and purchase a

small amount of cold tar (molasses works, too, but it remains sticky and attracts ants) and a small brush from your local hardware store. (Total cost around five dollars.)

If a student donates her doll, be sure she knows it will not be usable afterward. Recognize her to the class for her contribution.

Lay down protective paper or plastic. Paint the doll with the cold tar, then sprinkle the feathers over the sticky tar. Let all the students see the results, then hang the doll up as a reminder of the punishment some early citizens of our country endured.

Another idea is to give the tarred-and-feathered doll back to the student at the end of the school year, which she can then keep as her own reminder of our past. Recently, a former student of several years back told me she still has her tarred and feathered doll hanging in her garage.

Learn about the Roman Empire

Build the Parthenon. Add fake gun powder (flour) to symbolize the use of the Parthenon as an ammunition storage facility. For detailed instructions, see *http://school.discovery.com/lessonplans/programs/parthenon/*.

Science and Health Cooking

Prepare and cook a stew of small squid, octopus and frog legs dissected in science class. (For safety and health reasons, do not permit the students to consume anything cooked in class.) Make sure each student has his or her own small octopus or squid.

(These can be obtained from an Asian food market.)

Anatomy of a Tooth

Ask each student to bring a bar of inexpensive soap to class. (The bar soap brand Ivory works best for this project.) With round-tip paring knives supplied by the teacher, or special carving instruments with blunt tips, carve a tooth from the soap. (Some of my students' carvings were outstanding!) You can add beeswax and string to show nerves, if you want to take the lesson that far. Then see if a local dentist will display the carvings for a while, as a way of connecting with the community. Our local dentists were happy to accept my students' tooth carvings and they always took the best of the bunch.

Ahoy! Pirates!

There are several activities you can do that will teach students about the impact pirates had on society several hundred years ago. One is to have them make their own pirate flags, or jolly rogers. Another is to play a pirate game on the playground, using flour bullets – a tablespoon of flour wrapped in toilet tissue. Perhaps the most fun of all is to cook salmagundi, a popular pirate food usually consisting of just about anything that comes to mind (meat or chicken, grapes, anchovies, eggs, onions, you name it), served with oil and vinegar.

Little known fact: Pirates had a social security system and each ship crew included a preacher, a band and a doctor. Also, when pirates came upon alcohol on a captured ship, they did not immediately drink it; no, they used it to scrub the decks to kill bacteria and minimize illness. (Any of the potent stuff that remained was, of course, consumed.)

These activities motivated students to read the books *Robinson Crusoe* by Daniel Defoe and *The Swiss Family Robinson* by Johann Wyss. Some even checked out books about pirates from the library.

Playing Games

I used the fun game of Hangman and the long-time favorite table game of Monopoly to teach certain lessons. You can modify just about any well known game, including Clue, Old Maids card game, Trivial Pursuit, Pictionary and others.

Food Preservation the Early American Way

The Food Preservation exercise is best when broken down into five ten-minute special quick lessons or as a complete 50-minute program. It should be done in October or November at the latest, so the food can be preserved through the Winter and cooked in the late Spring.

Learning with Food Lessons

Be sure to visit my Warnings and Cautions chapter at the end of the book, especially if you plan to use food or cutting instruments in class.

Preserving Beef with Salt

Required Items for each class demonstration

1. Paper or cloth towels (for cleaning up)
2. A pan of water (for cleaning up)

3. Liquid soap (for cleaning up)

4. Four 1-lb boxes of granulated salt (any kind)

5. Two 2-inch deep rectangular or square cake pans (not round)

6. One cutting board

7. One non-serrated sharp knife for cutting the meat

8. One thinly-sliced piece of raw beef about the size of your hand and about one-fourth inch thick (for each class demonstration)

Directions:

1. The teacher cuts the meat into thin strips about six to eight inches long. Give the demonstration yourself as you tell your students how this preservation method was used by early American settlers.

2. Pick up one of the pieces of cut beef and pour salt on it. Do this over the empty pan, as you will use the salt later. Some of the salt will adhere to the sides of the beef.

3. When you have finished salting the beef, tell the students that you must saturate the meat with salt. Pinch the slice of meat hard, so you can feel your fingers through the meat. As you pinch the meat, you'll notice the salt becomes somewhat pink.

4. After pinching the beef, sprinkle enough additional salt into the pan to cover the entire bottom of the pan so that none of the pan is visible.

5. Lay the strip of salted meat into the pan on

top of the salt. At this point, if you have additional pieces of meat, ask volunteers to come up to salt and pinch them.

6. Cover the layer of meat with salt. Use the salt remaining in the box and one additional box.

7. Place the pan containing the beef and salt in a dry place. (Sometimes I place it on a table or window ledge where it will get sunlight, which helps to dry it.)

8. In a couple of days, the salt will have turned pink from the juices of the raw beef. Now transfer the meat into a second pan, following the same procedure in step 5 above. Do not discard the leftover salt in the first pan.

9. Stir the salt remaining in the first pan, to break up the lumps and enhance the drying process.

Notes:

•   Because of the salt, there will be no bacteria and flies will not be attracted to the meat in pan 2.

•   As time goes by, the salt will draw out the moisture from the meat.

10. Repeat steps 1 - 9 every three or four days for three to four weeks. Not changing salt pans on weekends is not a problem, as long as the meat is completely covered with salt to preserve it.

11. In about four weeks, remove the piece of meat from the salt.

12. Discard the salt.

13. After the meat is thoroughly preserved and consummable, prepare it for eating by washing it carefully several times in water or whole milk; or soak it until it becomes soft (several hours) and all the salt is disbursed into the liquid. Discard the liquid.

14. Fry the meat in cooking oil, margarine or butter.

Tip:

I like to hang the dried beef as a classroom decoration. To do this, get a strong length of string and a large needle. Skewer each end of the meat and tie the ends together. Hang the meat on the wall or bulletin board to remind the students of the methods used by our ancestors for keeping meat safe to eat. Be sure to tag it with a date.

All About Jerky

Several recipes for jerky, both soft and hard, have been practiced by different cultures throughout the world over the centuries. North American Indian tribes created pemmican, a soft jerky, by mixing dried ground meat with dried fruit or suet. Jerky, a hardened meat, is made by removing all moisture and heating the meat to at least 160°F.

When preserved properly, meat can last a long, long time and will be edible years later. I have given demonstrations to students using meat that was preserved as long as seven years previously.

Caution: For safety, legal and health reasons, do not let any student eat or taste any food you have used in a demonstration.

Preserving Sausage with Lard

Required Items for each class demonstration:

1. Cooking pan or electric skillet
2. Large-mouthed jar, about 56-60 ounce capacity, made of glass with a lid
3. Freshly ground sausage (about 2 pounds)
4. One large metal or wooden dipping spoon
5. Clean towels or paper towels for cleaning up
6. Soapy water for cleaning up
7. Goggles for students to wear (sometimes goggles can be borrowed from the Science or Industrial Arts department)
8. Lard (animal lard only) – about four or five pounds; enough to fill the jar (see #2)

Cautions:

Keep the students away from the cooking area. During student participation times, make sure the students are protected with goggles and aprons, etc.

Stan role-played the popular Rev. Mather of early day American history.

Tell the students that early Americans did not know about cholesterol, so they ate all of the fat and skin of the meat they cooked. They knew that some of the flavor came from the juices of the fat and they ate it with great pleasure. Yummy!

Animal fat had a utilitarian purpose for early Americans and people living in rural areas of our country in recent years, because the high temperature melting point of the fat (lard) provided excellent protection against bacteria and bugs. Because of its high temperature melting point, animal lard was better than vegetable lard.

Today, animal lard is difficult to find, so if you plan to conduct this exercise for your students, start your research early. Tip: You can usually find animal lard in Hispanic food markets. If you can't read the label, ask the proprietor or clerk if the lard contains animal fat. If it is not animal lard, do not buy it.

It may surprise you that the actual preservation of meat is very easy. Here's how:

Directions:

1. Set the glass jar out at least 30 minutes before beginning the demonstration, to allow it to come to room temperature. It should NOT be cold.

Once the jar is warm or room temperature ...

2. Wash your hands and have the students wash their hands.

3. Distribute paper towels and small tufts of sausage to the students.

4. Ask the students to make little sausage balls (about the size of a silver dollar).

   Before taking the next step, for safety, make sure the students are standing or sitting a distance away from the cooking area.

5. Heat the skillet until it is very hot.

6. Pour a small amount of the lard into the skillet, about one inch deep.

7. Remove the skillet from the burner (keep the burner on, but keep the children away from it).

8. Gently pour a small amount of the heated lard from the skillet into the jar, to about one inch deep. Be very careful to pour slowly. A sudden shock to the glass could easily cause it to crack and break, spilling its contents.

9. Place some of the students' sausage balls into the hot skillet on the burner, and roll them around until all sides of the balls are lightly browned.

10. Place the cooked sausage balls in the jar and cover with liquid lard from the skillet.

11. Repeat steps 9 and 10 until the jar contains about one to one-and-a-half inches of lard above the highest sausage balls.

12. Place the jar on a low shelf or in a cupboard where it cannot fall or be disturbed.

13. Have the students wash their hands well after working with the food.

The sausage balls are ready to eat, but they can also be stored for a long time and be preserved with the animal lard that covers them. When you're ready to eat them (for safety, health and legal reasons, do not permit the students to eat them), simply pour the sausage balls and lard into the skillet and cook away the grease. Cook until the sausage balls are thoroughly prepared and show a nice rich brown color. Turn off the heat, then remove the sausage balls carefully and lay them on paper towels to drain the grease. Yummy.

Preserving Eggs with Lard

Usually, it's best to perform this exercise in the Fall. You'll put the eggs away during their preservation process over the winter months, then return to the demonstration in the Spring to retrieve and cook them.

Required Items for each class demonstration:

1. Four or more fresh, uncooked eggs
2. Towels (for cleanup)
3. Soapy water (for cleanup)
4. Animal lard – about two pounds. (One pound is probably sufficient for five or six class demonstrations, but get two to be safe.)
5. A sheet of newspaper for each egg
6. Storage bucket, about five gallon capacity. (About $2 at the home improvement store)
7. Grain – about two pounds. (Grain such as wheat, rice or oats is used to support the eggs and keep them from breaking.)

Directions:

1. Conduct a teaching lesson before the experiment: Explain to the students that although you cannot see them, each egg contains millions of tiny, porous holes in its shell. In nature, as the baby chick develops inside, it

receives oxygen and releases carbon dioxide through the shell's pores.

Eggs used for this demonstration do not contain baby chicks, because the eggs have not been fertilized. The eggs were harvested commercially, not on a farm.

2. Have each participating student carefully take one of the fresh, uncooked eggs and, with the other hand, get some animal lard. With the lard, they'll play as if they are making a snowball. Show them how:

3. Rub the egg all over to fill the pores with lard. Make a coating that is about one-fourth inch thick all over the egg.

    Note: When the lard is applied, no oxygen can enter and no carbon dioxide can leave the shell.

4. Gently wrap the greased egg in a piece of newspaper. The newspaper will help support the egg so it will not break when placed in the bucket.

5. As the students are finishing, pour about two inches of grain into the bottom of the bucket. Ask each student to place his or her newspaper-wrapped egg on top of this first, lowest level of grain.

6. Pour about two more inches of grain into the bucket (enough to cover the newspapers and eggs plus at least one inch of grain).

7. Set the bucket aside in a place where it cannot fall, be kicked or disturbed and where it

will not be affected by heat or cold.

The eggs are now in a state of being preserved for future use, and you can leave them there for months. It is wise, however, to keep them in a cool place. The eggs can be protected without the grain (the shock absorber), but you must use more paper to absorbe shock in the event they are dropped.

Opening the wrapped eggs

When you are ready to cook the eggs (usually in the Spring):

1. Carefully remove each egg from its newspaper wrapping.
2. Crack each egg open into a warm skillet.
3. Study the egg shell to be sure it has not broken. Even a small crack can be a problem.
4. Inspect the egg yolk carefully. Be sure it displays a normal color and appears firm. A little fading to light yellow is fine. A brown yolk should be cause to discard the egg.
5. Inspect the egg white surrounding the yolk to be sure it is clear and gel-like.
6. Notice the smell of the egg. If it seems unpleasant or causes even the slightest hesitation about the egg's healthiness, discard the egg.

You can also test an egg for freshness by dropping it gently into a glass of water. If it floats, don't eat it.

Preserving Carrots with Sand

Our ancestors were so smart! They needed vegetables during the harsh winter months when growing them was impossible and there was no such thing as a supermarket! So they devised a way to preserve and enjoy their carrots year 'round.

Required items for each class demonstration:

1. A small bucket that is at least three inches deeper than the largest bunch of carrots plus 1.5 inches of carrot green tops
2. A bunch of carrots
3. Enough clean sand to fill the bucket

Cautions:

- Do not wash the carrots.
- Be careful not to break the skin of the carrot

Directions:

1. Fill the bucket with clean sand.
2. Trim the carrots' top greens to 1.5 inches in length.
3. Gently place each carrot into the sand, making sure that all of the carrot is covered.
4. Place the bucket in a safe, temperature controlled place, where it cannot fall or be disturbed.

In a few weeks or months (up to seven months), the carrots can be removed from the bucket, washed, scrubbed and eaten raw or cooked.

Making Butter

This is an "extra credit" project that's a lot of fun

and teaches children how early settlers and citizens enjoyed the benefits of fresh butter all year.

Grading the project:

- In keeping with the extra credit theme, points are awarded only to the student who brings the equipment, not by the student who acts as a helper). You will find that some students will not bring the requested supplies. This should not be a cause to lower the grade of the student. It only gives extra grade points to the student who brings the equipment.

- This is a great opportunity to help a student whose grades need a boost because of the effort he or she contributes to the project.

- You can assign all the credit points you would like; they do not need to be the same for every student. You can help the slower student's grade without hurting someone else's grade.

Required items for each class demonstration:

1. A clean, wide-mouth juice bottle of one pint capacity or more

2. One pint of warm whole cream (or enriched cream)

3. Small plastic refrigerator container with lid for taking butter home; or the jar they brought to class.

Directions:

1. Start the exercise at the beginning of class. (It will take about 40 minutes to get the butter

made.) Make sure the cream is lukewarm or room temperature when you begin (not hot, not cold).

2. Instruct the students to pour the cream into the juice bottle, leaving at least two-and-a-half inches of empty space at the top. Fasten the lid on tight.

3. Instruct the students to agitate the cream by tipping the bottles back and forth, slowly. Point out that rocking the bottles too rapidly will defeat the process and result in liquid, not butter.

4. Keep the agitating process going for 30 to 40 minutes. (Usually, butter will not appear before 40 minutes.)

5. After 30 minutes, if there is no sign of butter forming, pour a small amount of warm (warmer than room temperature) water into the cream, leaving a couple inches of space. Continue agitating.

Students who brought the supplies can share butter from their jars with students who helped agitate by having the helpers spread some of the butter in the little plastic containers.

Have the students leave their marked jars in your classroom until school is out. This way, the bottles won't get broken.

Tell the students that the butter is edible, but it must be salted for flavor (unless they prefer unsalted butter). When they uncover it at home, they should gently press a little salt into it until it is flavored as they like it. Serve it at dinner and report the family's reactions to the class the following day.

Points of Interest:

The pioneers traveling westward trails across America always had fresh butter. They milked the cows in the evening, put the cream in a sealed bucket and hung the bucket from the back of the covered wagon. As the wagon bumped along the rough trails and in-and-out of the ruts of wagons that had gone before them, on the way to California or Oregon, the cream agitated. By sunset of the next evening, they had fresh butter.

The liquid that remains after the butter is made is called buttermilk (or whey). The little creamy curds that didn't become butter are the curds. Remember the poem:

> *Little Miss Muffet*
> *Sat on a tuffet*
> *Eating her curds and whey.*
> *Along came a spider*
> *And sat down beside her*
> *And frightened Miss Muffet away.*

Let's Make "PE" Fun!

Usually, the boys are much better than the girls in physical education, but with a little imagination, girls against boys can really be fun. For example, give the girls a handicap and if it's great enough, they'll win or at least be equal.

Softball

Set up the playing field with four bases (not three)

and a home plate. The boys hit the ball and run to first base, then to second base and then to third. When they run to third base, however, it's deep in center field. Not many of the boys will reach fourth base.

Stan's students became acquainted with the Union Soldier on many occasions.

The girls will run the regular three bases and home. They'll learn quickly that after first, second and third are filled with boy runners, all they have to do is to get the ball to fourth for an easy forced out. The boys have fun, because they know it's just a game.

You can also make the rule that all boys except the pitcher and catcher must be at least ten feet behind the baseline. Of course, it's also fun to start moving the third base in a little closer to the original baseline with every inning.

Basketball

Put eight girls against five boys and tie a ribbon around each boy's writing hand. Play the game as usual, but don't allow the boys to use their ribboned hand for either shooting or dribbling. You'd be surprised how much fun this game can be for your students.

Boxingball

Boxingball is my name for this fun sport that I invented several years back. It uses five girls and five boys to play a regular basketball game with these exceptions:

Each boy's writing hand is ribboned.

The boys are not allowed to shoot or dribble the ball with the ribboned hand.

Each girl wears a boxing glove on one hand.

The girls may hit the boys with the gloved hand any time they want to, even if the boy does not have possession of the ball.

Foul shots? Hmmmmm. What is a foul? Of course, only boys foul.

The whole school will enjoy watching this game. I had the players of the Salvation Army Youth Center team, which I coached, play this game at a Los Angeles Lakers - Boston Celtics game and it brought the house down. It was so much fun that we got to play it at the half time of a University of Southern California vs Oregon State game in the Los Angeles Sports Arena. Both participants and spectators enjoyed the game.

An Idea for Your Health Class

In 1970, I was teaching a health class in which I discussed mental health and how people "scapegoat" to place blame on others for things they themselves do. (An example is the first baseman dropping a nicely thrown ball and blaming his drop on the sun, the wind or some other factor.

One day, I looked up from teaching to see the face of a beautiful sixth grader, Suzie Smothers, who was the daughter of comedian Dickie Smothers of Smothers Brothers fame. I asked Suzie if she would mind if I played a recording of one of her father's acts in class. She said it would be fine to use it.

Do you remember the Smothers Brothers television skit about, "Mom Liked You Best?" Well, I played that skit for the class and they went wild. And what an easy way to get a point across. I guess I must have played that part of

Let 'er rip, Stan!

the record at least 20 times that year. Even the students in Art class wanted to hear it.

Caution: Not all of the Smothers Brothers' skits are suitable for children, so preview everything you hope to present, especially the skits about John Henry, the Pilgrims and Johnny Appleseed, which contain adult material.

Test the Teacher Fun

Assign a chapter in history or a story from a reading class for the students to study. Instruct them to learn the material thoroughly, including every fact, picture, name, date and detail. Give them ample time to learn it well. Then ask the students to give you (the teacher) a test on what they learned. They may ask you any question relating to the assigned material. Questions such as "What's on page two, line three?" are not allowed. This is a great learning tool that generates a high level of interest in the class.

Multi-Subject Exercise for Teachers and Teams

This fun educational exercise teaches interpersonal relations and teamwork as well as three subjects. For this lesson, you'll work together with two teachers of other subjects. Your school principal will love this activity, as it uses three or more different learning disciplines. In the following example, I'll use history, art and English as the subjects.

In planning the lesson, each teacher selects a topic within his or her specialty area that will be covered.

- The history teacher selects a particular era or act of history.

- The English teacher selects a certain area, such as grammar, punctuation or parts of speech.

- The art teacher selects a technique, tool, medium or other special art area for learning.

- The Music teacher selects a tune, a series of notes or some other area of music.

During the planning phase, choose a teacher to

begin the lesson. This teacher will explain the process to the students when they are assembled in his or her classroom on the starting day. The entire exercise can take three days to complete.

Grading

Since the work is performed in teams, individual grading can be based on participation in the process and each student receiving the same grade as every other member of his or her team. (You'll see additional notes about grading as you read along.)

You can also arrange for the students to participate in the grading of projects submitted by other teams, but not their own team. If you do this, be sure they write their names on the backs of their papers, not on the front, so they will not assign highest grades to their friends.

Directions

The subject examples used in my directions may be changed to suit your teaching plan. For demonstration purposes, I've used the art teacher as the initiating instructor.

The exercise begins in the art class:

1. Divide the class into teams of two. (If you have a large class, three students to a group is also a workable number.)
2. Provide each team with construction paper and drawing tools.
3. Instruct each team to select one person as the "artist."

4. Instruct each team artist to draw a picture that represents an event or teaching point from let's say, the Civil War. Direct the team artist to draw a picture incorporating suggestions and ideas from the rest of the team.

5. At the end of this first session, tell the students to take their drawings with them to the next class that is participating in the exercise.

In the next participating class (music teacher in charge):

1. Ask the teams to sit together as they did in the first class.

2. Instruct the teams to select one person to be their songster.

3. Instruct the team songsters to create a song parody about the picture drawn in the first session.

4. Tell the teams to help their songster as much as possible with the tune and the words.

(A parody is a song in which the words are changed to match the music of a familiar melody. For example, "The Star Spangled Banner," written by Francis Scott Key during the War of 1812, is actually a parody of an old English pub song called, "To Anacrenon in Heaven.")

Although it's best if the students come up with their own songs to parody, this example of a short, easily identified tune might help them if they're having trouble getting started on this phase of the project. At the very least, it will serve as an example:

> Mary had a little lamb
> *Old Abe Lincoln went to war*
> Little lamb, little lamb,
> *Went to war, went to war*
> Mary had a little lamb
> *Old Abe Lincoln went to war,*
> Its fleece was white as snow.
> Our Civil War it was. (or Many a man was killed.)

Hint: Sometimes you can cheat a little, like making the word "Many" (in the last line) contain only one syllable.

The song-writing parody part of the project is the hardest, but not surprisingly, the kids have a great time doing it and usually every student participates. This project can be done totally as a self-contained history project. It works great that way.

Grading for the music section of the project

The best grade the group will receive will be a B+ equivalent credit, but it must be *extra credit points*. All members of the group will receive the same extra credit points unless the teacher sees that a certain student goofed off, hindered the group's progress or did nothing. If this happens, simply adjust each grade and explain to the students why you did so.

In the third participating class (English teacher in charge):

1. Ask the teams to sit together as they did in the first class.

2. Ask the teams to select one person to be their writer or poet. Let them make the decision, according to the skills present on their team, about whether that person will be a poet or writer.

3. For teams selecting a poet, instruct each poet to write a three stanza poem that speaks about the picture.

4. For teams selecting a writer, instruct each writer to write a one paragraph story about the picture.

5. Tell the teams to help their poets and writers do their work with proper punctuation, grammar, capitalization and sentence structure.

Student skill levels

Because some students may not have skills required for certain sections of this exercise, use this grade as an "extra point" grade. This way, the "A" students will not lose their perfect grades if they don't have that particular talent. Taking this approach means you will not receive some of those dreaded phone calls or emails from parents who just don't understand the reasoning behind the grades.

Praise, Praise, Praise

Be sure to praise the students who shine in this project. You'll find that some of your poorest students demonstrate talents you never imagined they had. And good for them! This may be the project they remember for a lifetime.

Praise the good work of individuals, as well as teams, in front of the whole class. They will love you for it. Spotlighting a child's natural talent, an ability that had been hidden or downplayed in the past, can easily change the direction of that child's life, inspiring the child to develop his or her skills in that area, to learn more and move in a positive direction. I've seen it happen more than once in my 33-plus years of teaching.

Survival Tips

I feel compelled to share some tips and observations I learned while taking survival school training during my stint with the United States Navy. They so fascinated me that I have shared them with my students and they were intrigued by them, too. Sometimes I talked to foods classes using these ideas, and that's why I'm including them here.

If you ever find yourself in a situation of fending for your life or having to devise ways to stay healthy or alive, remember:

- Your body needs moisture in order to digest food. If you have no moisture available, do not eat.

- Do not eat snow for water. The coldness of snow will cause great stomach distress. If you can, melt the snow. If you have no fire, find a container (such as a bottle or jar) in which to stuff some snow. Warm it up by holding it against your body.

- Use the broken end of a soda bottle as a

magnifying glass. Use the concave end of a soda can, which will reflect the sun's rays, to melt the snow.

- Watch wild animals and observe what they eat. Normally, whatever an animal eats can be consumed by a human. (This is not true of birds, which can eat berries that are poisonous to humans.)

- Avoid mushrooms unless you can confidently identify them as non-poisonous. Some mushrooms are deadly. Some have no calories. Since we need calories to stay alive, eating non-caloric mushrooms will do us no good.

- For the most caloric value, most meat should be eaten as raw as possible. This is NOT true of bear or pig (pork), which may have trichinosis worms or bacteria that can cause serious illness.

- If you are in doubt about the healthiness of meat you have killed for food, cook it until well done. Just be aware that cooking removes nutritional value, and it's nutritional value you need.

- The charcoaled crust of meat is not good for you. It contains no nutritional value and it probably contains carcinogens. Avoid eating it unless you really have no other choice or you need to throw up to eliminate some foul substance you may have consumed.

- Bugs, worms like nightcrawlers, snails, grasshoppers, crickets and the legs of frogs are all edible. (They taste better, of course, when cooked and seasoned.)

- Do not eat ants. (Other than specialty ants with chocolate covering!) Most ants have a protective acid in their bodies that will severely burn your mouth.

- If you must eat berries, roots and so forth (some of which can be poisonous), it is wise to eat just one berry first, then stop, move around for about 30 minutes and make sure that what you ate is not upsetting your stomach, making you sick or causing pain or any kind of distress.

- Should you drink the water? Pond water or creek water that is not moving is suspicious and probably not safe to drink. It's better to drink from rapidly moving water. If the water is dirty, try to strain it through your shirt to remove impurities. If possible, boil the water and let it cool before drinking it.

- Never drink ocean water. The salt content in ocean water is very high and will fiercely upset your digestive system and parch your throat. This heightens your need for food and fresh water. People have died from drinking ocean water.

  Trivia: It's interesting that the Amazon River in South America (the largest water volume river in the world) carries fresh water as far as 200 miles out into the Atlantic Ocean during the rainy season. This water, during this annual season, may be safely consumed.

- Can urine be consumed? Urine is mostly

water and relatively sterile. It's fine in an emergency, however, it does contain trace amounts of other substances such as alcohol, lead and arsenic. It should not be consumed in large quantities.

- Do not drink from the radiator of a vehicle, as radiators contain chemical-heavy anti-freeze.

- If you are lost anywhere in the world and you find human beings, it is a fairly safe bet that they will help you. My survival instructors taught that nine out of ten people, even in primitive areas and jungles, will help you. Those are pretty good odds.

Stan's Lesson Plan Comments

Hey, step out of the box! Let the kids do something different.

Really now, can't a math class do the lessons described in this chapter and throughout the book while working their problems at least one day of the year? Or how about a special education class or an English class?

Sure, they can! Will you be breaking any rules? Of course not!

Have some fun! It will make your day – and your students will love you for it!

Stan's Out-of-the-Box Stories

Having Fun with a Fellow Teacher

You may hesitate to do this, but your students will surely remember it (and so will the other teacher).

Ask a fellow teacher in the morning:

"Will it be alright if my students use your flag?"

Of course, the teacher will say, "Yes."

As soon as you are in your classroom, tell the students you are taking them to the other teacher's room to recite the flag salute.

Then do it. Lead the students into the other classroom and salute that teacher's flag together. Then just leave and return to your own classroom.

Your fellow teacher's mouth will still be wide open as you leave the room. If he or she says anything, just refer to the permission that was given earlier to use that flag.

You'll still be giggling at morning break.

Warnings and Cautions

Food Cautions

Some exercises published in this book make use of food and result in food dishes. Laws governing the preparation and serving of food and beverage have not been applied here nor has permission for consumption been obtained from school administrators or parents. For your protection and the protection of your students, do not allow any student to participate in any project by eating any of the food. This is extremely important.

I have eaten perfectly good food preserved using the methods I share in this book, methods I feel I have proven to be safe. There have been a few times when food I had prepared or preserved seemed questionable. When I was in doubt, I declined to eat it and I shared with my students the reasons for my hesitation. Early Americans used the same reasoning and decision-making process.

Using Tools and Cutting Instruments

For safety sake, do not allow any student to use a knife or sharp instrument.

Taking Exercises Too Far

In my first year of teaching, I decided to help my students understand the privileges that white slave owners' children enjoyed versus the obvious lack of privileges granted to the children of slaves. I divided the class into the two groups, one taking the part of the disadvantaged slaves' children and the other group representing the more privileged slave own-ers' children, for role playing. In two days, the roles were to be reversed. After only a day-and-a-half, the project fell apart.

The exercise was supposed to go on for four days but students' emotions got a bit edgy, so I ended it early. That was a tough call for me, but I felt it was too risky to the morale of the students to continue.

This sort of class project should not be attempted. If there's any doubt or hesitation about the exercise or its fairness to any student or student team, don't do it at all.

Exceptional Students

The Chun and Midu Stories

I was privileged to have two thoroughly gifted Asian students, Chun and Midu, whose IQs were probably in the upper 160 range.

Chun

Chun was the daughter of a Chinese mathematician who was considered the number two mathematician in China. Expecting to be imprisoned by the government, he escaped with his family. Later, when I asked him if he had a dream, what he'd like most to do, he said he wanted to measure the distance between the stars. Wow.

Chun excelled in school and was probably beyond the level of my sixth grade students in her own language and culture. There was hardly anything I could teach her in my sixth grade class. Her English was perfect, she knew history, she read like a news broadcaster and she knew all the math that our sixth grade book offered.

Because her maturity level was still that of a sixth grade student, I required that she do the same work her classmates did. She agreed. Then I introduced her to the school's computer. Before the year was over, this sixth grader finished the tutorial books in math, including those for geometry, first and second year algebra and half of the trigonometry program. She was a happy little girl who got to work alongside her classmates and enjoy challenges appropriate for her potential and ability.

Chun went on to Johns Hopkins University to study nuclear medicine. Unfortunately, out of fear of being identified by the Chinese government, her highly educated father continued to work as a dishwasher in a small local restaurant.

Midu

Midu came to my United States history class not knowing any English except Hi and Thank You. I gave permission to Midu and another Korean student to share notes, hoping that Midu would acclimate more easily and would learn from the student who had more familiarity with the English language.

At the end of the first trimester, both girls got As. They both continued to excel throughout the second trimester. I had a suspicion that Midu might be copying, but I was wrong.

About the middle of the third trimester, Midu began to speak up in class. Oh, my, what beautiful language she spoke! Her grade at the end of the third trimester was A+, and the grade of the other student, Midu's mentor, was B.

Midu was truly special and highly gifted. When her father visited the school, I learned that he had earned doctorates at Stanford University, University of California-Berkeley and Massachusetts Institute of Technology. He was in Southern California in order to be with his family while attending California Institute of Technology in Pasadena. In Korea, he had been named the country's Poet Laureate.

The following year, Midu was accepted at a prestigious girls school in Boston.

When teachers give a little freedom to students, it sometimes creates the opportunity that helps them excel. When truly gifted students and those who sincerely want to do well are encouraged, the rewards are great for them and you. Their success will bring tears to your eyes and loud thumps on your chest.

Hey, Midu and Chun ... I'm proud of you and hope you're doing well.

Stan's Out-of-the-Box Stories

Kel Ann: Our Special "Daughter"

My second year of teaching brought me in contact with Kell Ann, a pretty little girl who was very badly treated at home by her father. Kell Ann had a poor self image and her grade average was barely a D. Although her sisters and brother were great athletes and

the pride of her family and our school, Kell Ann walked with her head down and a defeated look on her sweet face. She rarely participated in activities with other girls on the playground.

One day, she asked if she could baby-sit my three small sons. I asked how much money she charged and she responded with a look that said, "What do you think? I want to do it for nothing."

Along came Friday, and I told her my wife Cheri and I would like her to come over at 6 p.m., but only if we could pay her. We would be gone until around 9 p.m. Kell Ann came to our house and we felt confident leaving our boys with her.

When we returned, we were pleasantly shocked. All three of the boys had been bathed and put to bed and she was reading a story to them. As we walked through the house, we noticed that all the toys were picked up and the dishes had been washed and put away. Cheri said, "Would you look at that? She even vacuumed the whole house."

For several years, Kell Ann came over to play with our kids. We noticed that her homework always got done and her grades continued to rise. Cheri asked if we might take her on vacations with us and, when Kell Ann's mother agreed, we did. But first, I requested that Kell Ann learn a poem and be able to recite it to me any time I asked. The poem is one I have assigned to my students as extra credit:

The Man Who Thinks He Can

If you think you are beaten, you are;
If you think you dare not, you don't.
If you'd like to win, but think you can't
It's almost a cinch you won't.

If you think you'll lose, you're lost,
For out in the world we find
Success begins with a fellow's will;
It's all in the state of mind.

If you think you're outclassed, you are.
You've got to think high to rise.
You've got to be sure of yourself before
You can ever win a prize.
Life's battles don't always go
To the stronger or faster man;

But soon or late the man who wins
Is the one who thinks he can.

By Walter D. Wintle, "The Man Who Thinks He
Can."— Respectfully quoted: Poems That Live Forever, comp. Hazel Felleman, p. 310 (1965).

With constant positive support, Kell Ann's attitude began to change. What a thrill it was to see her head held high and her self confidence soar. She moved in with us for about a year-and-a-half during high school and began calling me Dad. Sadly, when Kell Ann and her mother moved to Colorado, we lost track of her. Our attempts to locate her failed.

Then one day, I got a surprise phone call. The voice at the other end of the line asked, "Are you Mr. Cody, the teacher?" That was all I needed to hear. I knew Kell Ann's voice and I yelled, "Kell, I love you, tell me where you are." Well, she told me she was living in Colorado, was married, had two children, had earned both bachelors and masters degrees, runs 5K and 10K runs and marathons with her father-in-law and is now teaching mentally handicapped children. What achievements!

I know that the other thing I taught Kell Ann to do, while she had lived with us, had a lot to do with her astounding record of achievements: I asked her to look into her own eyes in the mirror every morning and say, "Kell Ann, I love you. Kell Ann, you are beautiful. Kell Ann, you will succeed."

Tears flooded my eyes when I spoke with her that day. She still calls me Dad, which just thrills me no end. And, Yes, I still get that "Yes, I Can!" from her.

I truly hope there is a Kell Ann in your life.

Bibliography / Resources

Here's a list of interesting books I've found useful in teaching United States history. Some would also be helpful in introducing ideas to other learning topics. I hope you find them as interesting and useful in making your classes fun as I did. Most of these books are available at online and local book retail stores.

American Heritage. By far, the best information I've found about American history comes from this group of periodicals. This multi-volume set of magazines can probably be found in your school library. It may also be on the selection list of magazines available for subscription, which students sell to raise funds at the beginning of each school year.

Don't Know Much about History (ISBN 0060083824), by Kenneth C. Davis, is truly outstanding. It also has a sister book, *Don't Know Much about Geography* (not quite as effective). Both books are available in book form as well as audio tapes.

***The Prairie Traveler: A Handbook for Over-
land Expeditions*** (ISBN 0918222893), by Captain
Randolph Barnes Marcy, was a bestseller guide for
pioneers crossing the continent in the 1800s. It gives
all sorts of information to aid the traveler on his
journey: reasons using mules is better and safer than
using horses, how to prepare beef jerky powder, how
to tell if horses are ridden by Indians or not, how to
handle Indians who come begging, and more.

***American Adventures: True Stories from
America's Past, 1770-1870*** *(ISBN 0962265217),*
***American Adventures: True Stories from
America's Past Part 2: 1870 to Present*** *(ISBN
0962265225)* **and** ***American Heroes: 1735-
1900*** *(ISBN 0962265225),* all by Morrie Greenberg,
are all available from Brooke-Richards Press. They
tell adventure stories that are not widely known and
they provide an excellent source of homework material.

***American History: The New York Public
Library Book of Answers*** (ISBN 0671796348),
by Melinda Corey, makes for interesting reading. It
includes the New York Public Library's most asked
questions (such as who was the first child born of
African parents in the American colonies) and shares
some very useful general information.

Chronicle of America *(ISBN 0131337459),*
by Clifton Daniel, published by Simon & Schuster in
1992. A very good book using a newspaper format
with news stories about everything from Columbus's
landing on the Island of Hispaniola in 1606 to
George Herbert Walker Bush's election in 1992.

Chronicle Of America: Colonial Times, 1600-1700 (ISBN 043905107X), by Joy Masoff, published by Scholastic Book Services. Re-creates early American settlements by describing in words and pictures various aspects of the colonists' lives including work, food, clothing, shelter, religion and relationships with native Americans.

The above book offers a lot of information. It's written like a newspaper story, describing events that happened in the early days of America in a timeline, journalistic style. J.L. International Publishing.

1001 Things Everyone Should Know About American History *(ISBN 0385244320),* by John A. Garraty, offers a fascinating reference that can be accessed randomly for specific dates and names.

1001 Facts Somebody Screwed Up (ISBN 1563520648), by Deane Jordan, offers interesting trivia and facts about America, including some which are a little contentious like Jordan's statement that there really are only 46 states in the United States since four "states" are actually commonwealths.

Knowledge in a Nutshell (ISBN 0966099184), by Charles Reichblum, shares amazing stories, trivia about American history and questions like: Do penguins have knees? Why do clocks run clockwise? Who put the butter in "butterfly?"

On-line Resources

http://eb.com - Encyclopedia Britannica site offering products and resources for schools and libraries *http://school.discovery.com* – a treasury of lesson plans and activities

http://www.wikipedia.org - a free encyclopedia that anyone can edit and add to

http://ushistory.org - lesson plans, examples and more

http://www.memoryelixir.com - intriguing memory tricks by Dr. Wilson

http://en.wikipedia.org/wiki/Mnemonic_major_ system - Explains the Major System, a famous mnemonic technique more than 300 years old, which aids in memorizing numbers.

http://www.betterendings.org/Homeschool/Fun/ mnemonic.htm - Definitions and examples of mnemonics and memory tools

http://www.sitesforteachers.com - reviews kids' websites, offers study tips

http://www.sitesforteachers.com - educational web sites rated by popularity

http://school.discovery.com/students - homework help and study tools

http://yahooligans.yahoo.com – Yahoo's educational games and sites

http://www.aolatschool.com – AOL's current events for students, educators and parents

http://www.brainpop.com - get homework questions answered, math, English, health, science, technology, social studies

A Little Story About the Author

Stanley (Zeke) Cody at age five.

Stan Cody (better known as "Zeke") grew up in the wonderful little prairie farming town of Nickerson in South Central Kansas. Stan's dad, Walt, was a driller in the oilfields who had quit school in the eighth grade to work and help his family. Stan's mother, Mildred Clark Cody, kept busy with church work and Girl Scouts, and his sister, Melba Cody Frank, excelled in school and enjoyed membership in the National Honor Society.

Not the studious type, Zeke played sports and chased girls. He likes to say that, at least, he was suc-

Stan (Zeke), second from right, top row, in 1954 with his eighth grade classmates and their all-time favorite teacher, Mr. Bollinger.

cessful in playing his favorite game of football.

Nickerson and its people were largely responsible, along with his family, for Stan's attitudes and his desire to excel. The population never reached more than 1,172, but the town was filled with loving, down-to-earth folk who were always willing to lend a hand. In the summer season when wheat was being harvested in the fields, people attended church in blue jeans and work clothes. If a farmer was ill or could not work, neighboring farmers brought their combines, trucks, sons and yes, even their daughters, to get the work done. Many times, these neighborly folk lent their hands to help another even before they harvested their own wheat. They even furnished their own gasoline. One special person, Brad Berridge, owner of the local IGA grocery store, furnished all the free sandwiches and soft drinks these thoughtful, caring people needed.

Teachers at Nickerson's school went out of their way to help their students and for that, Zeke Cody will always be grateful. He was a student who always had a smile on his face and a cheerful, "Hi, How Ya Doin?" He made "just good enough" grades so he could participate in athletics. Those Cs and D-pluses just weren't cutting it. He could have done better.

Zeke never read a complete book until he became a senior in high school. Childhood illness and other factors delayed his learning. The first book Zeke read from cover to cover was Dale Carnegie's *How to Win Friends and Influence People*. He still owns that book. As he grew and learned, thanks to the influence of caring, mentoring teachers, Zeke found his perfect occupation – being a teacher himself – and went on to earn many honors, including six Teacher of the Year awards.

If you asked Zeke today how he survived school without reading, he'd wrinkle up his nose, think about it briefly, and then say, "I guess I survived because I was a good listener, I never missed class and I was as creative as anyone could possibly be in order to remember things."

Upon entering Hutchinson Junior College, where he played two years of football, Zeke discovered that studying wasn't as tough as he'd thought it would be. And, of course, he'd read *How to Win Friends and Influence People* and a few more books. Having discovered his reading ability, he no longer resisted reading or studying.

Author Stan Cody

Zeke graduated with an Associate of Arts degree and then transitioned to George Williams College where he earned a Bachelor of Arts in Social Psychology. This YMCA Social Work School in Chicago offered him the opportunity to learn to understand people, games, human relations, society, psychology, party planning, love and creativity. In fact, he discovered how creative he really was. Zeke's time at George Williams College helped build

*An early picture
of Stan's children.*

a unique foundation for teaching in the years ahead.

After service as an officer in the U.S. Navy, the Urban Teachers Corp at UCLA accepted Zeke for graduate work. This led to his career as a successful, much honored and respected teacher. His teaching career paralled the wonderful years of raising a fine family: Christy, Skip, Scott and Steve, who all benefited from Zeke's out-of-the-box teaching memorics.

Zeke would like all his readers and students to know that the kind of creativity shared in this book is accessible to all of us. He invites you to send your comments about the book, as well as your ideas, school memories, mnemonics and memory tools and questions to him.*

Stanley Cody
25851 Treetop Road
Laguna Hills, CA 92653
Website: *www.StanCody.com*
Email: *stan@stancody.com*

*Material you submit is subject to publication in Mr. Cody's next book and website. If your material is published, proper credit will be given to you. Please provide your name, phone number and postal mail-

ing address (Your email address would also be helpful, so Mr. Cody can correspond with you, but it will
not be published.)

Coming Up!

In the future, you may enjoy Stan Cody's
Making History Fun and *Campfire Fun with
Pooky and Zeke*. Watch the website, *www.
stancody.com*, for updates.

Index

Index to Pictures & Illustrations

Available for
Speaking & Seminars

*Stan Cody as Benjamin Franklin, second
from left, with Buena Park, California
Rotary Club officers, after speaking to the
group in 2006.*

Bring Stan Cody's lively, entertaining presentations and characterizations to your faculty or group!

Topics

Teaching Out-of-the-Box Seminars
for School Faculties

The Forming of our Constitutional Rights,
featuring *Ben Franklin*

Early Pioneers and Heroes and Their Impact Upon
Our Freedoms Today, featuring *Daniel Boone*

For More Information

Stan Cody
25851 Treetop Road • Laguna Hills, CA 92653

Phone (949) 768-1928 • Email *stan@stancody.com*
StanCody.com

Send Stan Your Mnemonic-Memoric

Got a cool memory tip or mnemonic? Stan Cody would like to know! Submit your memory idea for consideration in Stan's upcoming books and website and get full credit.

Memoric Submission

Name _____

Address _____

City _____ St ____ Zip _____

Phone (_____) _____

Email _____

My mnemonic-memoric helps you to remember this:

Here is my mnemonic-memoric (Use a separate page if needed):

My Agreement. I understand that the memory aid I am submitting may be published in a Stan Cody book or website with credit given to my name as listed below; I further understand that Stan Cody Publishing will not share, sell or otherwise distribute my name, address, phone or email address for any other use unless I so indicate. Here is my name as I would like it published if my mnemonic-memoric if used:

Print clearly: _____

Signature: _____

Date: _____

____ Please notify me if Stan Cody publishes a new book or CD.

Mail To:
Stan Cody Publishing

Teaching
Out-of-the-Box

Teaching Out of the Box is a timeless guide to making learning fun for youth and adults.

We can customize books ordered in bulk for your school or organization with a gold label on the cover, with up to 20 characters of text. Upon request, the author will even autograph your books. We're open to other customization requests and we invite your inquiry about discounted bulk orders.

Order Form

Book:	Qty: ___	@ $16.95 USA	=	$ _____
	Qty: ___	@ $19.75 Canada	=	$ _____
Shipping/Handling:	$5.00		=	$ _____
Total:			=	$ _____

Please mail your check (payable to Stan Cody Publishing) to:

Stan Cody Publishing
25851 Treetop Road • Laguna Hills, CA 92653-5417

Be sure to indicate if you wish your book to be autographed.

More Details, Bulk Discounts & Customization:

Phone: 949 768-1928 • Email: *Stan@StanCody.com*

This information and an order form are available
at *www.StanCody.com*.

To order by credit card on the Internet:

www.Amazon.com